GROUNDED IN
TRUTH

VOLUME 1

A NINE-WEEK BIBLE STUDY ON THE ESSENTIALS OF
THE CHRISTIAN FAITH STRAIGHT FROM GOD'S WORD

FROM THE MESSAGES OF ADRIAN ROGERS

Grounded in Truth: Volume One (Bible Study)

Published by Love Worth Finding Ministries, Inc.
    2941 Kate Bond Rd
    Memphis TN 38133-4017
    (800) 274-5683

Copyright © 2023 Love Worth Finding Ministries, Inc. All rights reserved. No part of this publication may be reproduced, stored in a retrieval system, or transmitted in any form by any means, electronic, mechanical, photocopy, recording or otherwise, without the prior permission of the publisher, except as provided by USA copyright law.

This Bible study is taken from Pastor Adrian Rogers' message series, *Back to the Basics, Volume 1*.

Scripture taken from the New King James Version.® Copyright © 1982 by Thomas Nelson. Used by permission. All rights reserved.

Printed in the United States of America

CONTENTS

INTRODUCTION 1

WEEK 1
How Can I Be Certain About the Word of God? 3

WEEK 2
How Can I Be Saved? 17

WEEK 3
How Can I Be Sure I Am Saved? 31

WEEK 4
How Can I Know I Am Going to Heaven?................... 45

WEEK 5
How Can I Live a Spirit-Filled Life? 59

WEEK 6
How Can I Turn Temptations Into Triumphs? 73

WEEK 7
How Do I Deal With Sin in My Life? 87

WEEK 8
How Do I Restore Fellowship With God?................... 101

WEEK 9
How Do I Know God Is Working in My Life? 115

LISTEN NOW.. 128

DISCUSSION GUIDE 129

INTRODUCTION

GROUNDED IN TRUTH

Many people say they believe the Bible. They give lip service to the fact that the Bible is the inspired, inerrant, infallible, authentic Word of God. But they don't take the time to study it. They don't know what the Bible says, and they don't live by it. They don't assimilate it into their everyday lives, and when trouble comes, they don't stand on it. They don't have theology; they have me-ology. They live for right now and don't consider their eternal future. They follow their truth without knowing THE Truth. If we say that we believe the Bible, we must study it so that we can know that it is true.

It is absolutely imperative that you be certain about your faith. Until you get the basic truths of Christianity settled, you will not get much of anything else settled in your life. Despite what others may say, you can know for certain that you are saved through the truth of God's Word. When you trust Jesus, God is at work, making you more like Jesus, and using you in His kingdom. When you know the answers to questions about the essentials of the Christian faith, your life can be more of an exclamation point than a question mark.

Today, people question everything. Everything that is not nailed down is coming loose, and the devil is pulling up nails as fast as he can. In this study, we go back to the basics to help you get the truths of the Christian faith nailed down. When you know these truths, you will be secure in your faith. When you are secure in your faith, you have the opportunity to share the truth with others. Join us and become grounded in the Truth.

You don't have to check your brains at the door to believe that the Bible is the Word of God.

ADRIAN ROGERS

WEEK 1

HOW CAN I BE CERTAIN ABOUT THE WORD OF GOD?

INTRODUCTION

What do you believe about the Bible? There are those who simply hate God's Word. Some don't despise it; they just deny it. They don't believe the Bible is the Word of God. Others distort it and twist it to their own destruction. Some dissect it and come to the Bible with their measuring rods and their scalpels, bent on finding its shortcomings. They treat the Bible more like a math book than a love story. They are always learning but never able to come to the knowledge of the truth. Others disregard it and say it's not relevant or important. They say we should forget all of that religious hocus pocus. They don't have theology; they have me-ology—speak your truth, and I'll speak mine; live your truth, and I'll live mine. In reality, there is only one truth, God's truth, which He gave us through the Bible.

Are you certain that the Bible is God's Word? God's Word, written in the Bible, is truth, and your usefulness, your well-being, and your eternal destiny depend on it. If you want to live like an exclamation point rather than like a question mark, you need to be certain the Bible is the Word of God. This week we are going to look at the ways we can be certain the Bible is true.

PRAY OVER IT

Dear God, I want to be more certain of Your Word because sometimes I have doubts, and I'm bringing my doubts to You. Show me the truth about the Bible and give me the courage to live by Your Truth. Guide my thoughts and bring me a deeper understanding of who You are. In Jesus' Name, Amen.

DAY 1

SCIENTIFIC ACCURACY OF THE BIBLE

PONDER IT

The Bible itself claims to be the Word of God. It also gives a strong warning to anyone who would add or take away from it.

> **For I testify to everyone who hears the words of the prophecy of this book: If anyone adds to these things, God will add to him the plagues that are written in this book; and if anyone takes away from the words of the book of this prophecy, God shall take away his part from the Book of Life, from the holy city, and from the things which are written in this book (Revelation 22:18-19).**

God put in place many safeguards and assurances to guard His Words as they are written in Scripture. Therefore, we can know that the Bible is true. This week, we will learn several reasons we can be certain that the Word of God is true.

We can know the Bible is the Word of God because of its scientific accuracy. The skeptic will say that the Bible contains scientific errors. However, the Bible is not a science textbook. It was not given to tell us how the heavens go, but how to go to Heaven. The God of creation and the God of salvation are the same. Science doesn't take God by surprise.

The ancient Egyptians, the leading scientists of their day, thought the Earth was supported by pillars. The Greeks believed the Earth was held up by the back of Atlas, a mythical giant. In the Bible, we read what is true:

> **He stretches out the north over empty space; He hangs the earth on nothing (Job 26:7).**

Another scientific fact that the Bible proves is that the world is round. Even in Christopher Columbus' day, the greatest civilizations believed that the world was flat. Thousands of years before then, Isaiah spoke the scientific truth:

It is He who sits above the circle of the earth (Isaiah 40:22a).

In 150 BC, an astronomer named Hipparchus created a catalog of the stars. Hundreds of years later, Ptolemy, another astronomer, found even more stars. Later on, a young medical student named Galileo invented the first telescope. He found millions and millions of stars, disproving all the greatest minds who lived before him. Today, we know that there are countless stars that dwell within countless galaxies. The Bible told us this all along.

"As the host of heaven cannot be numbered, nor the sand of the sea measured, so will I multiply the descendants of David My servant and the Levites who minister to Me" (Jeremiah 33:22).

PUT IT IN WRITING

- What messages have you heard from the world about the relationship between the Bible and science?
- Have you ever had doubts about the validity of the Bible? Write them down. Then, write down a prayer, asking God to help you this week to trust Him by faith and learn more about why you can rely on His Word.

> Every now and then science may disagree with the Bible. Just give the scientists time, and maybe they will catch up.
>
> ADRIAN ROGERS

DAY 2

BIOLOGY IN THE BIBLE

PONDER IT

Biology is another aspect of science that gives us proof of the Bible's validity. Our bodies are living proof of God's fingerprint.

> **I will praise You, for I am fearfully and wonderfully made (Psalm 139:14a).**

For many centuries, people thought that illnesses were only concentrated in blood. Sick people would go to barber shops to be cut with razors because they thought the tainted blood would drain out. Many died as a result of this erroneous practice. The red, white, and blue stripes that swirl around poles outside of barber shops still remain to symbolize the procedure. We now know that there are some diseases that are housed in the blood, but we do not drain people's veins to treat them.

The Word of God says that life, not illness, is in the blood. No hematologist on earth can say it any better than God has succinctly said it:

> **"For the life of the flesh is in the blood" (Leviticus 17:11a).**

The Black Plague came to Europe in the fourteenth century. It desolated the population. An estimated sixty million died in the plague, and no doctor knew what to do. It was not the scientists who brought the plague to an end, but the Church. With no knowledge of microbiology, they gleaned from Moses' ancient writings in the Word of God, which taught the sick to quarantine.

> **"He shall be unclean. All the days he has the sore he shall be unclean. He is unclean, and he shall dwell alone; his dwelling shall be outside the camp" (Leviticus 13:46).**

A physician in Vienna, Austria, named Semmelweiss noticed that one in six pregnant women died from infection. Semmelweiss tried to find out what was wrong, and he noticed that the doctors were going from the morgue, where they would do pathological studies and post mortems and autopsies, straight into the maternal exam rooms...without washing their hands. They were spreading diseases and infections. Semmelweiss suggested that the physicians begin washing their hands before entering the exam rooms, and there was significant outcry among the doctors due to the inconvenience of taking extra time for another step in their duties. Yet, when they applied the new protocol, the death rate dropped to one woman out of 84. Now we understand why: there are microscopic organisms that spread infection, and we must wash our hands to prevent them from spreading.

In the Bible, God told us how to prevent infection, long before the discoveries of modern medicine. God gave Moses direction on what the Hebrews should do after handling wounds and dead bodies.

> **"The clean person shall sprinkle the unclean on the third day and on the seventh day; and on the seventh day he shall purify himself, wash his clothes, and bathe in water; and at evening he shall be clean" (Numbers 19:19).**

Centuries before modern technology and medical practices, God taught the concepts of quarantining, bathing, and allowing time for bacteria to die. The discovery of germs did not take God by surprise. Modern science confirms what God's Word has taught for millennia.

PUT IT IN WRITING

- How does today's message encourage your faith? What stood out to you?
- Do you look to Scripture to confirm what you learn in your life, or vice versa? How did today's reading challenge your approach?

When you believe the Bible, it is not a leap into the dark, it is a step into the light.

ADRIAN ROGERS

DAY 3

HISTORICAL ACCURACY OF THE BIBLE

PONDER IT

We can have confidence in Scripture because of its historical accuracy. Just like the Bible is not a science textbook; it is also not a history textbook. Even still, it accurately records history.

The first five books of the Bible were written by Moses. Some scholars believed that people in his time were illiterate, so it would have been impossible for Moses to be an author. But then in 1887, ancient clay tablets were discovered in Northern Egypt. We now call these tablets the "Amarna letters." They were writings that described business transactions between Egyptians and Palestinians from centuries before Moses was born. Not only did the people of Moses' time know how to write, but they had a postal system.

In Daniel 5, the author described a feast at which the king of Babylon, Belshazzar, witnessed the fingers of a man's hand writing words of prophecy on the wall. For centuries, archeologists couldn't find records of a Babylonian king named "Belshazzar," so they concluded that the Bible was wrong. But in 1854, archeologists discovered evidence of Belshazzar in four unearthed, ancient texts called the "Cylinders of Nabonidus." Belshazzar was the son of Nabonidus, the co-ruler of Babylon at the time. This is why it makes sense that Belshazzar deemed Daniel the "third ruler" of the kingdom.

Scripture confirms history, and many archeological facts confirm Scripture. But even if relics were not discovered, God's Word would still be true.

PUT IT IN WRITING

- What does it say about God's character that the Bible is historically accurate?
- What should believers do when they hear claims that the Bible is not historically accurate? How does it change the argument when you come to the Bible believing that it is historically accurate?

> The Bible is not the book of the week; it is not the book of the month; nor is it the book of the year. It is the book of the ages!
>
> ADRIAN ROGERS

DAY 4

UNITY OF THE BIBLE

PONDER IT

We can have confidence that the Bible is the Word of God because of its unity. The Bible is one book, but it contains 66 books: 39 books in the Old Testament and 27 books in the New Testament. These books were written by at least 40 different authors over a period of about 1,600 years. They were written in 13 different countries and on three different continents by people of varied backgrounds. The authors were shepherds, kings, soldiers, princes, priests, fishermen, scholars, and historians. Some were business and professional men, and others were common laborers. The Bible contains information written on countless subjects in three different original languages. Yet, even with multiple authors in multiple locations and time periods, it reads as one book from Genesis to Revelation.

The Bible is like a garment. You can pull a thread from the top, and it wrinkles all the way to the bottom. Read the Bible your entire life, and its unity will confirm your faith time after time.

The Bible has but one theme: salvation. The Bible has one hero: Jesus. It has one villain: the devil. Its one purpose is to glorify God. Jesus himself said that the Scripture cannot be broken (see John 10:35). The united Holy Scriptures were written by divine inspiration.

Here is an illustration someone gave about the unity of the Bible: suppose the United States decided to build in Washington a monument to the fifty states, made up of native rocks from each location. There would be coral from Florida, granite from Georgia, limestone from Tennessee, and so on. The rocks would be all different shapes, sizes, and colors. Imagine that each completely different stone could interlock to create a beautiful, symmetrical temple. It would be nearly impossible for all those stones to fit together by mere happenstance. It would have to be done on purpose by the work of a master architect.

The Holy Scripture is God-breathed, eternal, united, and intentional. On every page, we see the redemptive story that has its fruition in Christ. The Apostle John wrote about this:

> **In the beginning was the Word, and the Word was with God, and the Word was God. He was in the beginning with God. All things were made through Him, and without Him nothing was made that was made. In Him was life, and the life was the light of men. And the light shines in the darkness, and the darkness did not comprehend it (John 1:1-5).**

Everything written in Scripture fits together for the purpose of God's glory and our instruction. By design, though it covers a variety of subjects and historical time periods, it is cohesive and complete.

PUT IT IN WRITING

- Why do you think God chose to use multiple authors to write His Word? What is the purpose of the diversity within the unity we see in Scripture?
- What are some biblical themes you see that are consistent across the entire Bible? What do we see about God's character in every book?

The Bible addresses one problem—sin.
The Bible has one villain—Satan.
The Bible has one hero—Jesus.
The Bible has one purpose—to glorify God.

ADRIAN ROGERS

DAY 5

FULFILLED PROPHECY AND LIVING QUALITIES OF THE BIBLE

PONDER IT

We can have confidence in the Bible because the prophecies have come true. The Word of God contains hundreds of fulfilled prophecies.

Over three hundred prophecies about Jesus in the Old Testament are fulfilled in the New Testament. Statisticians confirm the impossibility that they were fulfilled by random chance. Consider these Old Testament prophecies that came true in the New Testament:

- He would be born of a virgin (Genesis 3:15)
- He would be born of the Seed of Abraham and bless all nations (Genesis 12:3)
- He would be a Lamb without blemish, living a perfect life (Exodus 12:5)
- Not one of His bones would be broken (Numbers 9:12)
- He would be cursed by hanging on a tree (Deuteronomy 21:23)
- He would be of David's lineage (2 Samuel 7:12)
- He would be betrayed by a friend, not an enemy (Psalm 55:12-14)
- He would be born in Bethlehem (Micah 5:2)

Jesus gave all of these prophecies and arranged their fulfillment thousands of years before He was ever born. Most importantly, He arranged that he would come out of the grave that third day. Many of the 500 people who saw Him after His resurrection confirmed this to their own deaths, with nothing material to gain, because they were no longer afraid of death.

Many men will live for a lie, but none will die for it. Fools may die for a lie when they think it's the truth, but these people were convinced that Jesus Christ had come out of that grave. His followers would not have knowingly died for the sake of a lie. In fact, most of the Messianic prophecies were fulfilled by those who would gain from them *not* being fulfilled. We have undeniable proof that Jesus was the Messiah and that Scripture is the Word of God.

We also know that the Bible is true because of its ever-living qualities. No book has ever had as much opposition as the Bible. Men have laughed at it, scorned it, ridiculed it, made laws against it, and burned it. Yet, the Word of God has survived, and it is still applicable today.

> "But the word of the LORD endures forever" (1 Peter 1:25a).

We know the Bible is God's True Word because it changes lives. We read other books, but this book reads us. It is the only book that is saving for the sinner, sanctifying for the saint, sufficient for the sufferer, and satisfying for the scholar. It is a bottomless ocean of knowledge, wisdom, comfort, instruction, and answers to life's problems. People read His Words and transform into versions of themselves that are not possible without the work of the Spirit.

> For the word of God is living and powerful, and sharper than any two-edged sword, piercing even to the division of soul and spirit, and of joints and marrow, and is a discerner of the thoughts and intents of the heart (Hebrews 4:12).

PUT IT IN WRITING

- Do you believe the Bible is the Word of God? Why or why not? If not, what else would it take for you to believe?
- Which role of Scripture applies to you this week: saving for the sinner, sanctifying for the saint, sufficient for the sufferer, or satisfying for the scholar? Why?

> The Scriptures are shallow enough for a babe to come and drink without fear of drowning and deep enough for theologians to swim in without ever reaching the bottom.
>
> ADRIAN ROGERS

DAY 6

CERTAINTY IN THE WORD OF GOD

PRACTICE IT

All of the Bible can be summed up in these well-known words: "Jesus loves me, this I know, for the Bible tells me so!" God loves you, and we can be certain of that through His Word. The Bible tells us that Jesus left Heaven, came to Earth, suffered, bled, and died for your sin. It says that God raised Him from the dead, and He is ascended to Heaven. Salvation is a gift of grace, and you can have it if you will trust Him. The same Jesus who fulfilled hundreds of prophecies two thousand years ago will save you and keep you according to the Word of God, the Bible.

Do you know that if you died today you would go to Heaven? If you do not have assurance of your salvation, the Bible says that Christ can save you. If you trust Him, you will be with Him one day in Heaven.

If you want to be saved, pray this prayer:

Dear God, I'm a sinner. I'm lost and I need to be saved. Jesus, I believe You are the Son of God. I believe You paid my sin debt on the cross. I believe it according to your infallible Word. I believe that You were raised from the dead, and now like a child, I lay my pride in the dust and trust You. Thank you for saving me. Help me never to deny You. In Jesus' Name, Amen.

If you are convinced that the Bible is true, then it must affect the way you live. One of the greatest enemies of the Word of God is a person who gives lip service to the Bible but does not live by it. If you believe it is the Word of God, you must study it, know it, live by it, assimilate it, and stand on it. In these days when everything that is not nailed down is coming loose and the devil is pulling nails as fast as he can, you must stand on this Book. God has given you the Word of God; it's time to live like it matters.

PROCLAIM IT

If you feel like this week of study has stirred up more questions than answers, take some time to talk with your pastor about what you are struggling with. There are many more examples of the scientific and historical accuracy of the Scriptures than we could share here. Take the time to research and discern the truth of God's Word. Your pastor can point you to more resources for you to explore that might give you a different perspective.

If there is something you learned this week that someone in your sphere of influence would benefit from hearing, pray and ask God to give you an opportunity to share. Ask God to give you the courage to speak the truth when the time is right.

If you prayed to receive Christ, please share your decision with another Christian you know or with your pastor. We would also like to hear about it, so that we can provide you with free resources to help you grow in your new faith. Please let us know by going to **lwf.org/discover-jesus**, scrolling down the page and clicking on *I Believe*.

> You will never be strong until you begin to feed on God's Word.
>
> ADRIAN ROGERS

> In a strange sense, doubt is a backward affirmation of faith. You only doubt that which you believe.
>
> ADRIAN ROGERS

WEEK 2

HOW CAN I BE SAVED?

INTRODUCTION

A woman was on her deathbed at the hospital, and her family sat in the waiting room, very concerned about whether or not she would go to Heaven. As they discussed their worries, a man overheard their conversation and asked, "May I have an opportunity to speak with her and tell her how to be saved?"

"Sure," they said.

When he entered the woman's hospital room, he asked, "Would you like to be certain that you are saved and going to Heaven?"

"Yes, I really would, but nobody can truly know if they are saved," she said.

The man let her know that she could indeed be saved and be certain of it. He shared words of truth from the Bible that solidified her faith.

When the man shared the news of her profession of faith with the family, her son-in-law said, "No one can know that they're saved. The best that a person can do is to hope that they are saved."

But God does not want us to live life with this uncertainty. He wants us to know for certain that we are saved. When we get back to the basics of how to be saved, our faith can come alive in new ways as we renew our gratitude for what Jesus did on the cross. It reminds us to live lives that reflect our relationship with Him.

PRAY OVER IT

Dear God, Thank you for sending Your Son, Jesus, to die in my place. I want to know for certain that I will spend eternity with You. Show me this week the ways I can know that I am saved. Show me how my daily life should reflect what I believe. In Jesus' Name, Amen.

DAY 1

THE ETERNAL DESTINY OF THE SOUL

PONDER IT

The Bible tells us that if we are saved in Christ, we never have to worry about our eternal destiny.

> **And this is the testimony: that God has given us eternal life, and this life is in His Son. He who has the Son has life; he who does not have the Son of God does not have life. These things I have written to you who believe in the name of the Son of God, that *you may know that you have eternal life*, and that you may continue to believe in the name of the Son of God (1 John 5:11-13, emphasis added).**

John did not say that we should "hope," "think," "guess," or "wonder." We can "know" that we have eternal life. We are not called to have a hope-so faith, but a know-so faith, living by the power of the Holy Spirit, who dwells inside of us. If you are a Christian, you have been redeemed by His blood; this changes your eternal destiny forever. As Christians, we have complete assurance that we will be in Heaven with Jesus when we die. Do not live as a question mark; live as an exclamation point.

Though we can trust the Lord completely, most of us would admit that we have doubts from time to time. God is so good that He allows us to have doubts. If we were not allowed to have doubts, the Apostle John would have had no reason to write these verses. If you have doubts, it does not mean you are not saved. Doubt is to your spirit what pain is to your body. It doesn't mean you are dead; it means something is wrong. As a matter of fact, dead people don't feel any pain.

In a strange sense, doubt is a backward affirmation of faith. You only doubt that which you believe. Let John's words that you can know that you have eternal life give you peace and assurance when you do have doubts.

In order to be certain that you are destined for Heaven, you must be assured of your salvation. It doesn't matter what church denomination you are affiliated with, what political opinions you hold, or what is on your resume. Eternal destiny is about your soul. When God made you, He breathed into your nostrils the breath of life and you became a living soul. Your soul will go on endlessly. It could no more cease to exist than God Himself could cease to exist. But your soul will live on in one of two places: either in Heaven or in Hell. Therefore, it is so important that you absolutely know that you are saved. This week, we will learn what the Bible says about how to be saved and what that means about our lives here on Earth.

PUT IT IN WRITING

- Have you ever doubted your salvation? Why or why not? How does what you learned about doubt today impact you?
- Does it matter if we know what happens after death? Do people today live as if their souls will live on forever, either in Heaven or in Hell? How would it affect your daily life to know for certain where you would spend eternity?

> We are not called to have a hope-so faith, but a know-so faith.
>
> ADRIAN ROGERS

DAY 2

WORKS-BASED GOSPEL

PONDER IT

If we want to know whether or not we will be in Heaven after we die, we must first ask the most important question: how are we saved? The Apostle John gave us the answer.

> **Whoever believes that Jesus is the Christ is born of God (1 John 5:1a).**

"Born of God" is another way of saying "saved." It means that you are born again. John made it plain and clear: the way you are saved is by believing that Jesus is the Christ. The name "Jesus" means "Jehovah saves," which makes Him the Messiah, the Savior of the world. When you trust and believe that, something happens in your soul, and you are saved.

> **So they said, "Believe on the Lord Jesus Christ, and you will be saved" (Acts 16:31a).**

The word "believe" doesn't mean just intellectual agreement with the facts. Even the devil believes like that. It is a word that means trust and commitment. The Apostle Paul explained this in his letter to the Ephesian church:

> **For by grace you have been saved through faith, and that not of yourselves; it is the gift of God, not of works, lest anyone should boast (Ephesians 2:8-9).**

God left no room for salvation to be attained on our own merit. Anyone can be saved, regardless of physical or intellectual strength. Paul made it very clear; self and works cannot save. It is only by grace through faith that we are saved. God gave salvation as a free gift to all.

It may seem like a simple concept, but many people hope they will go to Heaven because they are doing the best they can. Some also believe they will be saved because they are basically good people. But both of these ideas reflect a works-based gospel, and it is not what the Bible tells us is true. If we had to depend on our own actions to get to Heaven, none of us would be saved. God's holiness demands a perfect righteousness that none of us can attain through good deeds.

The average person depends on self and works to get into Heaven. How will such people know they have done enough? They can't know! They can only hope that when judgment comes, their good deeds outweigh their bad actions. But that works-based gospel is no gospel at all.

PUT IT IN WRITING

- Have you ever believed or lived like your salvation was based on your good works? What does the life of someone who hopes good works will lead to salvation look like?
- What does the life of someone who is saved by faith and grace look like? Why do you think God gave us the free gift of salvation rather than making us work for it?

> I wouldn't trust the best fifteen minutes
> I ever lived to get me into Heaven.
>
> ADRIAN ROGERS

DAY 3

SALVATION BY GRACE THROUGH FAITH

PONDER IT

Faith is not an intellectual agreement with facts or trusting in your good works. Today, let's learn what faith *is* because Paul said that salvation is by grace through faith.

> **For by grace you have been saved through faith, and that not of yourselves; it is the gift of God, not of works, lest anyone should boast (Ephesians 2:8-9).**

If we want to understand salvation, we must first understand grace. Grace is the unmerited favor and love that God shows to sinners. It is what made God love us when we were unlovely. God doesn't love us because we're valuable; we are valuable because He loves us. He loves us out of His grace. It is what sent Jesus to die for us when we were still sinners.

If you have trouble remembering what grace is, remember this acrostic:

    G - God's
    R - Riches
    A - At
    C - Christ's
    E - Expense

Similarly, we can remember faith this way:

    F - Forsaking
    A - All
    I - I
    T - Trust
    H - Him

Intellectual belief is only part of faith. Faith is also trust and commitment. By His grace, we can have saving faith if we choose it. Grace is the hand of God reaching down from Heaven to say that He loves you and wants to save you from eternal Hell. Faith is your hand reaching up to God. When you put your hand of faith in God's hand of grace, that's salvation. By grace, we are saved through faith.

The devil doesn't want you to understand that. He wants you to think that salvation is part of what you do and part of what God does. If any part of it depends upon what you do, you will never have assurance because you'll always wonder if you are doing enough. This is where the devil moves in and brings shame, sin, and separation from God. But when it all depends on what God does, then you can have assurance that you are saved. It is not about self-confidence, but confidence in the grace of God.

Though we can be certain of our salvation, the devil doesn't give up easily. He will try to convince you that it's partly grace and faith, but it's also partly your good works. You do your part and God will do His. He makes it sound as if you and God are a team, working tirelessly to drag you into Heaven, and if you ever mess up, the whole deal is off. This is a plot of Satan. Salvation is accomplished not by your works, but by Jesus' finished work on the cross.

And if by grace, then it is no longer of works; otherwise grace is no longer grace. But if it is of works, it is no longer grace; otherwise work is no longer work (Romans 11:6).

Salvation is not part grace and part works. It is all grace. You are saved when you admit that you are a sinner, that you are lost, and that you cannot save yourself. You trust Jesus to save you and you come under His authority. No one deserves or doesn't deserve to be saved because of what he or she has done. The Bible says whoever believes that Jesus is the Christ is saved.

PUT IT IN WRITING

- How would you define grace and faith to someone else? What does this look like in your own life?
- What is the benefit of being saved by faith and not by works? How does this affect how Christians live their lives?

DAY 4

THE LORDSHIP TEST

▪ PONDER IT

Though salvation is a free gift, believers have birthmarks that signify their second birth. We can boil all of these markings of our faith down to three assurance tests. In 1 John, the author wrote the word "know" almost 40 times. He gave us many ways we can be certain we are born again and the Holy Spirit is doing work in our lives.

The Lordship test: Is Jesus Christ the Lord of your life?

> **Now by this we know that we know Him, if we keep His commandments. He who says, "I know Him," and does not keep His commandments, is a liar, and the truth is not in him (1 John 2:3-4).**

Notice that John didn't say that we are saved by keeping His commandments. He said that we are confident that we know Him *if* we keep His commandments.

This does not mean that we never break His commandments. We have all failed and sinned at some time or in some way after we've been saved. John understood that.

> **If we say that we have not sinned, we make Him a liar, and His word is not in us (1 John 1:10).**

> **My little children, these things I write to you, so that you may not sin. And if anyone sins, we have an Advocate with the Father, Jesus Christ the righteous (1 John 2:1).**

The standard God sets for us is not to sin. But God is gracious, and He knows we fall short at times. That is why He gave us an advocate through Jesus. Jesus already paid the penalty for our sin, and He also continues to help us cleanse our lives from the lingering temptation to continue sinning.

On one hand, the Bible says we know that we're saved because we keep the commandments. On the other hand, it says it is possible for us to sin. The word "keep" is a word that sailors used to describe the way they navigated their ships by looking to—keeping—the stars at night.

As children of God, our stars are the commandments of God—what we steer our lives by. A sailor might get distracted or blown off course, but when he recognizes it, he resets his course and gets back on his way. Similarly, sometimes we take our eyes off of God. We steer off course and fail with remorse, but our desire is to keep God's commandments. If that is not the desire of your life, you need to be saved.

You are not saved by God's commandments, but by God's grace. But one of the birthmarks of being saved is a desire for Jesus to be your Lord. That's the Lordship test. Jesus said:

> **"But why do you call Me 'Lord, Lord,' and not do the things which I say" (Luke 6:46)?**

You cannot accept Jesus as your Savior and not make Him your Lord. It is impossible.

PUT IT IN WRITING

- Is Jesus the Lord of your life? How do you know?
- When you sin, do you feel remorse? Do you have a desire to keep God's commands? What does this say about your faith?

> Before I got saved I was running to sin. Now, I'm running from it.
>
> ADRIAN ROGERS

DAY 5

THE FELLOWSHIP AND RELATIONSHIP TESTS

PONDER IT

The fellowship test: Do you love your brothers and sisters in Christ? John had a lot to say about the way Christians should interact.

> **We know that we have passed from death to life, because we love the brethren. He who does not love his brother abides in death (1 John 3:14).**

> **If someone says, "I love God," and hates his brother, he is a liar; for he who does not love his brother whom he has seen, how can he love God whom he has not seen (1 John 4:20)?**

When you love the heavenly Father, you love His children. You love your brothers and sisters in Christ. When you get saved, you want to be right with other Christians.

Some people say they can worship God all by themselves and that they don't need church. But the Bible says not to forsake assembling together (see Hebrews 10:25). Throughout Scripture, God tells us that to love Him is to love others.

Fellowship is a test of your salvation because when you are saved, you become a partaker of the divine nature. Love is the nature of the Christian because it is the nature of God. God's nature is love, and you are to love others.

> **Beloved, let us love one another, for love is of God; and everyone who loves is born of God and knows God (1 John 4:7).**

Fellowship is also the nature of the Church, the people of God. The Bible calls the Church the body of Christ (see Romans 12:5). Just like each part of the body is essential for it to function properly, each of us plays a necessary part in God's Kingdom. You need to play your part in a community of faith.

The relationship test: Do you have a relationship with Jesus? When people get married, their time together does not end at the wedding. It is a life-long relationship. Similarly, we don't just have a one-time experience with Jesus; we actively believe in Him in the present tense. It is an ongoing relationship.

Your relationship with God is a present reality. Your faith is not just theology; it is a relationship. You're not saved by the plan of salvation, but by the man of salvation. Your life is in Jesus.

> **And this is the testimony: that God has given us eternal life, and this life is in His Son. He who has the Son has life; he who does not have the Son of God does not have life. These things I have written to you who believe in the name of the Son of God, that you may know that you have eternal life, and that you may continue to believe in the name of the Son of God (1 John 5:11-13).**

Your relationship with God now is more important than your relationship with God when you got saved. The gift of salvation is incredible, but the joy of our faith does not end there. It is an ongoing, living, active relationship. The proof of your faith is in your relationship with Christ today.

PUT IT IN WRITING

- Do you love your brothers and sisters in Christ? Are you regularly spending time with other believers? Why or why not?
- Do you have a relationship with Jesus? What does it look like right now? Does He feel more like a close friend, or more like an acquaintance?

> God's will for you is not a roadmap; it is a relationship.
>
> ADRIAN ROGERS

DAY 6

HOW TO BE SAVED AND KNOW IT

PRACTICE IT

God gave us an invaluable gift by allowing us to be certain of our salvation. When we accept Jesus as Lord and Savior, a river of peace runs through our hearts. In that moment, we can have assured hope that we will spend eternity in Heaven with Jesus Christ.

If you have accepted the free gift of salvation by God's grace through faith in Christ, your life overflows with obedience to His commands. You obey, not as an act of obtaining your own salvation, but as a display of joy and gratitude for what Jesus already did for you. You maintain close fellowship with like-minded believers, encouraging one another and building up the body of Christ. Lastly, you have a relationship with Jesus. Salvation is not a "one-and-done" experience; it is a life-long relationship with your Lord and Savior. It is personal and life changing.

If you have had serious doubts about your salvation, or perhaps you haven't understood the free gift of salvation and you have tried to work to earn it, you can set your mind straight today. You can truly know that you are saved, and rest assured that you will spend life after death forever with Jesus in Heaven. Confess your sin, and give everything to Him. Make Him the Lord of your life and seek to obey His commands. Tell Jesus that you believe whole-heartedly in His life, death, and resurrection. Then, thank Him for the assurance of your salvation.

PROCLAIM IT

Share with another Christian what God has taught you this week. Ask that person to keep you accountable to make any changes you need to make in your life.

If you know people who do not know for certain they are saved, ask God to give you opportunities to share with them what you have learned this week. Ask God to give you the words, the wisdom, and the courage to speak at the right time and in the right way.

If you don't have a church home, pray and ask God to help you find a church body that you can join. Look for a church that preaches the Gospel and values God's Word.

If you prayed to receive Christ, please share your decision with another Christian you know or with your pastor. We would also like to hear about it, so that we can provide you with free resources to help you grow in your new faith. Please let us know by going to **lwf.org/discover-jesus**, scrolling down the page and clicking on I *Believe*.

Salvation doesn't come from following the life of Christ but from receiving the death of Christ.

ADRIAN ROGERS

God is not a wishy-washy parent. His love and His promises do not waiver.

ADRIAN ROGERS

WEEK 3

HOW CAN I BE SURE I AM SAVED?

INTRODUCTION

As you learned last week, you can know for certain that you are saved. But there is something even more wonderful than that: knowing that once you are saved, you can never lose your salvation.

If you believe in Christ, you can have assurance that your salvation is eternally secure. You never need to wonder if it will fall away or worry that God will let you out of His care. This belief is fundamental to our faith, our confidence in Christ, and our evangelism. We must know for certain what the Bible says about this topic.

Jesus gave us this promise:

> **"My sheep hear My voice, and I know them, and they follow Me. And I give them eternal life, and they shall never perish; neither shall anyone snatch them out of My hand. My Father, who has given them to Me, is greater than all; and no one is able to snatch them out of My Father's hand" (John 10:27-29).**

PRAY OVER IT

Dear God, Am I secure in my salvation? I confess that I sometimes doubt my security. At times, I even fear that, one day, You might let me slip away from my faith. But Your Word tells me that I am eternally secure from the moment I believe. Help me to know my salvation is secure in You and to live out the courage and hope that brings. Thank you for loving me no matter what, and for keeping Your promise to me. In Jesus' Name, Amen.

DAY 1

IMPORTANCE OF ETERNAL SECURITY

PONDER IT

Eternal security in Christ is not incidental; it is fundamental. It is necessary for your spiritual health.

Imagine a young boy in a family. One day, his parents use tender and encouraging words toward him, causing him to feel loved and safe. The next day, they use cold and angry words, don't give him physical affection, and tell him he is no longer a member of the family. He feels afraid, confused, and abandoned by the change in his parents' temperament.

This type of treatment has lasting traumatic effects on a child, and no good mother or father would treat a child this way. In the same manner, we can feel great distress if we feel uncertain in our spiritual standing. If we couldn't know that we are saved and secure, we would lack the emotional stability that children of God should have. God is not a wishy-washy parent; He is a good Father and loves us more than any earthly parent ever could. His love and His promises do not waiver.

> **"I will be a Father to you, and you shall be My sons and daughters, says the Lord Almighty" (2 Corinthians 6:18).**

In addition to emotional and spiritual stability, our confidence in our eternal security causes us to be productive, fruit-bearing Christians. When you know that your future is secure, you can concentrate on the present.

In 1933, builders began construction on the Golden Gate Bridge. At the time, it was the world's longest suspension bridge. As they prepared to build it and calculated the costs based on industry norms at the time, it was projected that the $35 million-bridge would also cost 35 lives from workers falling off of the bridge. However, chief engineer Joseph Strauss demanded worker compliance with the latest safety precautions and also built a net that stretched under the bridge. Even with these precautions, 11 men died during construction, but 19 lived after falling into the net. They also found that productivity increased by 25% because the builders had greater focus knowing they were safe. It is the same with God's children. When we know that our future is secure, we can concentrate on the kingdom work in the present.

Eternal security is important in evangelism and soul-winning. Some people choose not to become Christians because they are afraid that they will not hold onto their salvation. They think they don't have the strength to "be good" or the wisdom to keep up with other Christians. They don't think they have what it takes to live like believers, and so they don't get saved at all to avoid falling away. These people let fear stand in the way of the best decision they could ever make. God saves, and He keeps those He saves.

PUT IT IN WRITING

- Have you ever questioned your eternal security? If so, what caused your doubts? What do you hope to learn this week to become more confident in your salvation?
- If you were completely confident in your eternal security, what do you think would change in your life? Be specific.

> Security is not in a place,
> but in a Person—Jesus.
>
> ADRIAN ROGERS

DAY 2

DEFINITION OF THE BELIEVER

▪ PONDER IT

Before you can be sure of your eternal security in Christ, you need to know if you are saved. A believer is not simply a person who has head-knowledge of the Gospel. It's not someone who has joined a church, has been baptized, gives a tithe, and takes part in other religious rituals. These things are good, but they do not save us. Salvation comes when a person receives Christ by faith. As a partaker of the divine nature, he or she has been twice-born and can never again be a lost soul.

Many of us can think of people we thought were saved but who do not seem to be any more. They have fallen away from living a life in line with God's Word. Often we think people are saved, but in reality, they never truly believed the Good News of Jesus Christ and were never actually saved. Only God knows what a person truly believes.

Jesus spoke about final judgment and described many of those who will appear to be saved:

> **"Not everyone who says to Me, 'Lord, Lord,' shall enter the kingdom of heaven, but he who does the will of My Father in heaven. Many will say to Me in that day, 'Lord, Lord, have we not prophesied in Your name, cast out demons in Your name, and done many wonders in Your name?' And then I will declare to them, 'I never knew you; depart from Me, you who practice lawlessness'"** (Matthew 7:21-23)!

Notice that Jesus didn't say that He used to know them but they lost their salvation. He said He never knew them. They might have participated in many outwardly religious things, but Jesus never knew them. He was not speaking about people who truly profess and believe that Jesus Christ is Lord and Savior. Remember what Jesus said:

"My sheep hear My voice, and I know them, and they follow Me. And I give them eternal life, and they shall never perish; neither shall anyone snatch them out of My hand" (John 10:27-28).

Though people may have been baptized, attended church, and lived lives that resembled those of true believers, those who "fall away" were never truly saved from the beginning. If they go away and stay away, they were never saved. The Bible tells us this is true.

They went out from us, but they were not of us; for if they had been of us, they would have continued with us; but they went out that they might be made manifest, that none of them were of us (1 John 2:19).

John said that these people didn't lose their salvation; they never had it from the start. Judas never lost his salvation; Judas was never saved (see John 13:8-11). Jesus knew from the beginning that Judas did not believe in Him. Eternal security is not for people who were never truly saved; it is for people who have had a personal, vital relationship with God through Christ.

PUT IT IN WRITING

- Who is someone in your life who appeared to be a Christian but "fell away"? Commit to praying for that individual throughout this week.
- Describe your journey of becoming a Christian. How has God given you assurance of security in Him?

> The faith that fizzles before the finish had a flaw from the first.
>
> ADRIAN ROGERS

DAY 3

PROMISE, PERSEVERANCE, AND PREDESTINATION

PONDER IT

We can be certain that we are eternally secure if we believe in Christ for three reasons.

God promised you eternal security. Paul gave us a list of many mighty opponents that cannot separate you from the love of God. If you die, you're still in the love of God. If you're still alive, you're still in the love of God. No earthly or spiritual power can separate you from the love of God. Nothing that happens can separate you from the love of God. Absolutely nothing changes the infinite love of God toward you. The Bible gives us this promise.

> **For I am persuaded that neither death nor life, nor angels nor principalities nor powers, nor things present nor things to come, nor height nor depth, nor any other created thing, shall be able to separate us from the love of God which is in Christ Jesus our Lord (Romans 8:38-39).**

God's love will persevere; He will complete what He has begun. When you got saved, you did not do the work inside your heart—God did. We love Him because He first loved us. He was the One who called us.

> **...being confident of this very thing, that He who has begun a good work in you will complete it until the day of Jesus Christ (Philippians 1:6).**

The Holy Spirit of God is the agent of the new birth, and He was the one who convicted you of sin. He showed you that you were a sinner and needed to be saved. He also opened your eyes and helped you understand the Gospel. He is the convictor, the converter, and the completer. We often start things we can't finish—books, projects, and plans. But this is not the nature of God. Jesus is able to finish the work that He started in you; His Word promises that He will do so.

God predestined those who are saved to be with Him forever. The Bible says that God knew in advance who would spend eternity with Him. When God foreknows someone, He predestines them. He gives them a destiny—a certain future in Heaven.

> **For whom He foreknew, He also predestined to be conformed to the image of His Son, that He might be the firstborn among many brethren. Moreover whom He predestined, these He also called; whom He called, these He also justified; and whom He justified, these He also glorified (Romans 8:29-30).**

God gave you a chain in these verses with five golden links: foreknowledge, predestination, calling, justification and glorification. If you're a child of God, God already sees you glorified and in Heaven. According to the Bible, when you believe, you are already glorified. If you are already predestined to be like Him, you cannot lose your salvation.

What is settled in eternity cannot be undone in time. God never changes His mind. If you are in Christ, God predestined you to be like Him and with Him in eternity.

PUT IT IN WRITING

- Which reason for your eternal security from today stands out to you? Why?
- Where do you see the Holy Spirit working in your life right now? What is the "good work" He has done in your life?

> What has been decreed by Heaven
> cannot be annulled by Hell.
>
> ADRIAN ROGERS

DAY 4

PERFECTED AND POSITIONED

PONDER IT

If the three reasons from yesterday weren't enough proof, we are going to add two more reasons that we can be certain that we are eternally secure if we believe in Christ.

Christ's blood has perfected you forever. Jesus' single, perfect offering—his precious blood poured out on Calvary's cross makes you perfect forever.

> **For by one offering He has perfected forever those who are being sanctified (Hebrews 10:14).**

When you get saved, God doesn't make a down payment and expect you to keep up the monthly installments. If you are in Christ, you have been made perfect in God's sight. You got more than a fresh start; you were given a new nature.

No one in the Bible was saved twice. It is impossible to be saved twice; just like it is impossible to be physically born twice. If you could be saved twice, Jesus would have to die twice.

Even though we are perfect in God's sight, it doesn't mean that we behave perfectly. Our flesh still exists, and on this Earth, we will always struggle with sin. We can disobey God, but when we do He disciplines and teaches us (see Hebrews 12:6-8). But our salvation, our perfection in His eyes, is not based on our good works, but on His finished work (see Romans 4:5-8).

You are already positioned in the Lord Jesus Christ. Those who are in Christ are made new. What is true of Jesus is true of all those who are saved. You are part of His body.

> **Therefore, if anyone is in Christ, he is a new creation; old things have passed away; behold, all things have become new (2 Corinthians 5:17).**

Noah's ark is more than just a story of a great ship; it is a picture of the Lord Jesus Christ. God didn't tell Noah to hang onto the outside of the ark during the storm to test him to see if he had the strength to be saved. God knows we don't have the strength to save ourselves. God didn't say, "Go into the ark." Instead, He invited Noah to come inside (see Genesis 7:1), and then God Himself sealed the door. The Bible says that when we respond to His invitation and step into a relationship with Jesus, we are sealed by the Holy Spirit (see Ephesians 1:13).

The only way that Noah could have gone down would be for the ark to go down. The only way for me to lose my salvation is for Jesus to go down, which will never happen. Noah may have fallen down many times in the ark, but he never fell out of the ark. In the same way, we as Christians can slip, stumble and fall, but we do not lose our salvation. Just like Noah was secure inside the ark, we are secure in Christ.

PUT IT IN WRITING

- How does the knowledge that God views you through Christ's perfection affect your posture toward Him?
- How would you describe your position in Christ? What are the benefits of this position? What parts are difficult for you to accept or believe?

> Noah may have fallen down many times in the ark, but he never fell out of the ark. In the same way, we as Christians can slip, stumble and fall, but we do not lose our salvation.
>
> ADRIAN ROGERS

DAY 5

POSSESSION, PRAYER AND POWER

PONDER IT

Today we add two more reasons that we can be certain that we are eternally secure if we believe in Christ.

When you are saved, you already possess eternal life. Jesus didn't say that you will receive eternal life; you already have it. It is not something you get when you die; you possess it the moment you believe.

> "Most assuredly, I say to you, he who hears My word and believes in Him who sent Me has everlasting life, and shall not come into judgment, but has passed from death into life" (John 5:24).

Jesus is praying for you. Jesus, who the Bible calls our High Priest (see Hebrews 4:15-16) who intercedes for us, said this about His disciples:

> "I pray for them. I do not pray for the world but for those whom You have given Me, for they are Yours. And all Mine are Yours, and Yours are Mine, and I am glorified in them. ...I do not pray that You should take them out of the world, but that You should keep them from the evil one. ...I do not pray for these alone, but also for those who will believe in Me through their word" (John 17:9-10, 15, 20).

Jesus Christ prays that you will be kept from the evil one, and He has never prayed an unanswered prayer. He always prays in the will of God, and God always hears Him. Jesus prayed for Peter this way:

> And the Lord said, "Simon, Simon! Indeed, Satan has asked for you, that he may sift you as wheat. But I have prayed for you, that your faith should not fail; and when you have returned to Me, strengthen your brethren" (Luke 22:31-32).

Though Peter stumbled and fell, he was the mighty Apostle of Pentecost. Peter was eternally secured through the power of Jesus' prayer, and so is every person who believes in Him.

Therefore He is also able to save to the uttermost those who come to God through Him, since He always lives to make intercession for them (Hebrews 7:25).

You are kept by the power of God. You are eternally secure by His power and have no reason to doubt that you will be with Him in Heaven.

Blessed be the God and Father of our Lord Jesus Christ, who according to His abundant mercy has begotten us again to a living hope through the resurrection of Jesus Christ from the dead, to an inheritance incorruptible and undefiled and that does not fade away, reserved in heaven for you, who are kept by the power of God through faith for salvation ready to be revealed in the last time (1 Peter 1:3-5).

There is no greater power than God's because nothing can pluck you from His hand (see John 10:27-28).

PUT IT IN WRITING

- What does it mean to you that a person receives eternal life the moment he or she believes? What do you have to do to get this gift of salvation?
- How does knowing that Jesus is praying for you impact your relationship with Him?
- Do you believe God is powerful enough to keep you from being taken away from Him? Why or why not?

> Death is only a comma to a Christian—not a period.
>
> ADRIAN ROGERS

DAY 6

HOW CAN YOU BE SURE YOU ARE ETERNALLY SECURE?

PRACTICE IT

The power of Hell is no match for the keeping power of Christ. Not even you can separate yourself from the love of the Father. No power is stronger than God's power to secure your eternal destiny with Him.

If you want eternal security, you must first know the Gospel and believe it. You need to say "yes" to the cleansing power of Christ's life, death, and resurrection. Give your heart to Jesus and the same God who saves you will keep you. If you have salvation, you have eternal security in Christ.

If you would like to be sure of your eternal destiny with God in Heaven, you can be saved today. Repent of your sin that has separated you from the Father, and accept the free gift of salvation through Jesus' blood payment on the cross. Believe in Him, and know that you will be secure forever by His power.

PROCLAIM IT

Share with a trusted friend or mentor the assurance of eternal security that resonated the most with you this week. If there are still reasons you doubt or question your security, talk with a Christian friend or pastor.

If you prayed to receive Christ, please share your decision with another Christian you know or with your pastor. We would also like to hear about it, so that we can provide you with free resources to help you grow in your new faith. Please let us know by going to **lwf.org/discover-jesus**, scrolling down the page and clicking on *I Believe*.

> You've got a Savior, not a probation officer.
>
> ADRIAN ROGERS

God's Word never contradicts itself.

ADRIAN ROGERS

WEEK 4

HOW CAN I KNOW I AM GOING TO HEAVEN?

INTRODUCTION

The topic of eternal security is so important that we are giving it two weeks in this study. In the first week, we considered eight reasons those who believe in Christ can be certain of their eternal security.

If you are truly saved, you accept Jesus as your Savior and Lord, submitting your heart to His will, and you take on a new, divine nature. As a new creation, you cannot go back to the old man. Your salvation is certain. What God deemed eternal cannot be changed.

But there are still some hard passages of Scripture that may cause us to question whether or not we can lose our salvation. When you see a supposed contradiction in the Bible, you need to explore its context and examine it carefully. God's Word never contradicts itself. Some passages of Scripture might seem to indicate that a person can lose salvation, but if we look closer, we can understand the true meaning. This week, we will look at these difficult passages and learn how they actually affirm our eternal security in Christ.

PRAY OVER IT

Dear God, When I still struggle with the same old sins, I question whether or not my faith is real. I begin to doubt that I will spend eternity in Heaven. Other voices and teachings in my life have told me that eternal security is not real. This week, open my eyes to see the Truth of Your Word. Help me to know that because I believe in Your Son Jesus I will spend eternity with You. Give me courage to share this message with others. Help me to live by faith and not by fear. In Jesus' Name, Amen.

DAY 1

A DOG AND A HOG

◼ PONDER IT

People might use this passage to teach that a person can be saved and be lost again. If you look closely, it actually teaches the exact opposite message.

> **For if, after they have escaped the pollutions of the world through the knowledge of the Lord and Savior Jesus Christ, they are again entangled in them and overcome, the latter end is worse for them than the beginning. For it would have been better for them not to have known the way of righteousness, than having known it, to turn from the holy commandment delivered to them. But it has happened to them according to the true proverb: "A dog returns to his own vomit," and, "a sow, having washed, to her wallowing in the mire" (2 Peter 2:20-22).**

In verse 20, Peter described people who changed their habits after hearing the Gospel. However, the passage never says that they received Christ, became new creations, and were saved. They learned about the Good News, likely from the lips of false teachers who did not lead them in truth. They escaped sin temporarily, but then they became entangled again because they lacked the transformative power of the Holy Spirit.

It is better for you not to know the way of truth than to make outward changes without truly knowing Christ. Judas is an example of this. Jesus said that it would have been better if he had never been born (see Matthew 26:24). Judas heard the truth and became a disciple of Jesus. He escaped the pollution of the world for a while, but he ultimately ended up in Hell.

Sinful desires do not disappear by reformation; they only hibernate and wake up stronger. That's what Peter's words meant. Salvation, on the other hand, gives you a new nature that desires not to sin.

Another reason we know this passage does not refer to someone who has been saved is because Peter compared these people to dogs and hogs. Nowhere in Scripture are children of God compared to dogs or hogs. The proverb means that though the dog felt better and the hog (a sow is a female hog) looked better for a while, neither truly changed what they were.

In Luke 15, the story of the prodigal son gives us an example of a true believer who wandered away from a righteous life. He ended up in a pig pen, but he knew he didn't belong there and wanted to return home. He knew he wasn't one of the pigs. He returned to his father's loving care.

In the same way, the child of God doesn't belong in the pig pen, he belongs in his Father's house. When people are truly saved, something inside of them tells them that what they are doing is wrong. Peter's warning was for those who experienced reformation without regeneration.

PUT IT IN WRITING

- Based on today's passage, is it possible for people to look and act like they are saved without truly being saved? How do the stories of the prodigal son and of Judas help us understand this concept?
- How would you describe the difference between reformation and regeneration? How have you experienced this in your own spiritual journey?

Reformation without transformation leads to greater degradation and final condemnation.

ADRIAN ROGERS

DAY 2

HE WHO ENDURES TO THE END

PONDER IT

Many people will use Matthew 24 to say that in order for you to be saved, you have to endure to the end. But God teaches that in order for you to endure to the end, you have to be saved. If you want to see who is saved, watch to see who endures.

> **"Then many false prophets will rise up and deceive many. And because lawlessness will abound, the love of many will grow cold. But he who endures to the end shall be saved"** (Matthew 24:11-13).

We only endure because God puts the ability to do so in our hearts. We don't hold onto Him; He holds onto us.

A father crossed the road with a son. Traffic was heavy, so the father told the little boy to hold his hand. The little boy's hand was so small that he wrapped it around his dad's index finger. As they crossed the street, cars approached faster than the dad anticipated. He took his finger out of the little boy's fist, grabbed his hand, and dragged him across the street as quickly as he could. When they came to the other side, the little boy said, "I held on, daddy!" In reality, the dad was holding onto the boy. Just like this boy, we who are saved endure to the end. We do not endure in order to be saved, but because we are saved. God saves us, keeps us, and sustains us.

Peter himself is another example that people use to say that we can lose our salvation.

> **And the Lord said, "Simon, Simon! Indeed, Satan has asked for you, that he may sift you as wheat. But I have prayed for you, that your faith should not fail; and when you have returned to Me, strengthen your brethren"** (Luke 22:31-32).

Jesus prayed that Peter's faith would not fail because his faith already existed. Jesus prayed that Peter would have endurance, and he did. Peter was frightened and cowardly when he denied Jesus. But God transformed his heart, and his faith proved to be true when he confessed his faith in Jesus once again. After the resurrection, Jesus asked Peter if he loved Him, and Peter affirmed his love three times (see John 21:15-19). Though he outwardly denied Jesus in a moment of weakness, he never forsook Christ inwardly.

Eternal security is like a strong rubber band that God puts around you when you get saved. You may stray away, but He keeps drawing you back. That is the strength of God's love.

PUT IT IN WRITING

- Have you ever looked back on a season of life and realized that God was holding onto you? How did you know that He was holding onto you?
- Have you ever outwardly denied Jesus like Peter? Have you received forgiveness and been restored like Peter?
- Write down these stories in your spiritual journey because they are important to remember. God may even give you an opportunity to share them with someone else.

> We are not saved *because* we endure;
> we endure because we are saved.
>
> ADRIAN ROGERS

DAY 3

HE WHO DOES NOT ENDURE

PONDER IT

Based on outward behavior, if you had to choose whether Peter or Judas was actually saved, you might think it would be Judas. Peter was a mess. He struggled with his faith and challenged Jesus several times in the Gospels. But Judas was the treasurer; the disciples trusted him. None of the disciples suspected that Judas would betray Jesus, but he did. Jesus invited Judas to follow Him even though He knew what would happen.

> "But there are some of you who do not believe." For Jesus knew from the beginning who they were who did not believe, and who would betray Him (John 6:64).

> Jesus answered them, "Did I not choose you, the twelve, and one of you is a devil?" He spoke of Judas Iscariot, the son of Simon, for it was he who would betray Him, being one of the twelve (John 6:70-71).

> And while He was still speaking, behold, a multitude; and he who was called Judas, one of the twelve, went before them and drew near to Jesus to kiss Him. But Jesus said to him, "Judas, are you betraying the Son of Man with a kiss" (Luke 22:47-48)?

Jesus chose Judas to be His disciple with His eyes wide open. He knew Judas would never believe, but He invited Judas into His circle so that the Scriptures would be fulfilled about the one who would betray Him. Even though Peter stumbled along the way, he ultimately endured in his faith. Judas fell away because he never truly believed.

Those who walk away for a time do not lose their salvation, but those who do not return and endure have failed the test of their salvation: it never existed to begin with.

In John's Gospel, Jesus spoke a parable:

"I am the vine, you are the branches. He who abides in Me, and I in him, bears much fruit; for without Me you can do nothing. If anyone does not abide in Me, he is cast out as a branch and is withered; and they gather them and throw them into the fire, and they are burned. If you abide in Me, and My words abide in you, you will ask what you desire, and it shall be done for you. By this My Father is glorified, that you bear much fruit; so you will be My disciples" (John 15:5-8).

Some might say that Jesus used this illustration to say that those who were once saved could fall away and be cut off from Christ, but in this passage, Jesus was not referring to salvation. He was talking about fruit-bearing for those who have already believed.

When vinedressers trim grapevines, they burn the useless trimmings. In Jesus' illustration, if a Christian doesn't abide in Him, he is good for nothing. He wasn't talking about Heaven and Hell, but about a person's usefulness in the Kingdom of God, the fruit of his life.

PUT IT IN WRITING

- What does it tell you about Jesus that He chose Judas to be a disciple even though He knew what would happen? What do you see as the main differences between Judas and Peter?
- What does it mean to you to "abide in Christ"? What does being connected to the true vine look like in your life? What was the fruit that grew out of Peter's life? What fruit do you see in your life?

> We do not lose our salvation when we sin. But if we persist in sin, we will lose the joy of our salvation.
>
> ADRIAN ROGERS

DAY 4

EYES WIDE OPEN

▪ PONDER IT

Some people believe that Christians can lose salvation, and if they do, they can never receive it back. In other words, instead of believing "once saved, always saved," they believe, "twice lost, always lost." They use Hebrews 6 to say that someone who is a wholehearted believer in Christ, who has been transformed by the Holy Spirit's internal work, and who rejects faith for a time, cannot ever return.

> **For it is impossible for those who were once enlightened, and have tasted the heavenly gift, and have become partakers of the Holy Spirit, and have tasted the good word of God and the powers of the age to come, if they fall away, to renew them again to repentance, since they crucify again for themselves the Son of God, and put Him to an open shame. For the earth which drinks in the rain that often comes upon it, and bears herbs useful for those by whom it is cultivated, receives blessing from God; but if it bears thorns and briers, it is rejected and near to being cursed, whose end is to be burned. But, beloved, we are confident of better things concerning you, yes, things that accompany salvation, though we speak in this manner (Hebrews 6:4-9).**

In this passage, the author is not addressing Christians. In verse 9, he drew a contrast between those he wrote about in the passage and those who are actually saved. He was not speaking about believers, but about those who come to the threshold of salvation and ultimately turn away. The Holy Spirit gripped their hearts and did everything to get them ready to accept salvation. They read the Word of God, were enlightened with the truth, and had eyes wide open, but they chose to reject Christ. Therefore, it is impossible for those who have fully understood salvation to be saved if they reject the truth. It is impossible for their hearts to come to true repentance because they don't believe.

A person who rejects Christ with eyes wide open is like a shopper at the grocery store who approaches a sample table. She tries an exquisite and rare cheese, the best she has ever tasted. It is so good, she decides to purchase two pounds of it. In the checkout line, she discovers that the price for the cheese is much higher than she expected. Rather than taking the product, she leaves it at the register and walks away. She rejects the best flavor she has ever tasted because the cost is too high.

People who reject Christ with full knowledge of the Gospel are like this woman. They understand the incredible, free gift they are offered, but the cost of giving up their sin is too high. They choose to walk in their own way, trusting their wisdom more than God's truth.

PUT IT IN WRITING

- What did God use in your spiritual journey to help you understand the truth of the Gospel?

> **When you're saved, God doesn't fix you so that you can't sin anymore, but you can't sin and enjoy it.**
>
> ADRIAN ROGERS

DAY 5

WORTH LIVING AND DYING FOR

PONDER IT

Imagine a plot of ground. One side has one type of seeds sown into it, and the other side contains another. A fence goes between the two portions of land. Both receive the same amount of rainfall and sunshine. On one side, the most magnificent fruit and vegetables spring forth from the ground. On the other, thorns and briers rise up, useless and ugly. The only difference between the two plots is the type of seed that was planted. This is the illustration we see In Hebrews 6:

> **For the earth which drinks in the rain that often comes upon it, and bears herbs useful for those by whom it is cultivated, receives blessing from God; but if it bears thorns and briers, it is rejected and near to being cursed, whose end is to be burned. But, beloved, we are confident of better things concerning you, yes, things that accompany salvation, though we speak in this manner (Hebrews 6:7-9).**

People can sit and listen to the same words and hear the same message of Christ's life, death, and resurrection. They hear the Word of God and feel the Holy Spirit stirring in their hearts, convicting them of sin and leading them to repentance. Some receive the Lord's gift of salvation; others, after hearing the same Gospel, reject it. People cannot be saved without the seed of faith in their hearts.

Hebrews was written to Jewish people, who were transitioning from living by Old Testament Law to life under the New Covenant. Many Jews struggled with going back to their old, familiar ways of maintaining their righteousness by keeping the law. When they professed their faith in Christ and stopped keeping the strict traditions of the Law, they were rejected by their families and persecuted. Some were even martyred. Many Jews who knew the truth about Christ turned their backs on Him because they were afraid and did not want to die. They were persuaded by the Jewish leaders to reject Christ after they professed faith. They were unwilling to give up what society offered them—a good reputation, safety, and comfort—for the sake of something much better: eternal life in Heaven with Jesus Christ. They knew the truth, yet denied it under pressure, committing an unpardonable sin.

A person who is truly saved cannot deny Christ in this way (see Hebrews 6:9). Those who have accepted salvation in Jesus Christ have confidence that the Gospel of Jesus is worth living for and dying for, and they endure to the end.

PUT IT IN WRITING

- Before you were saved, what held you back from believing? What did it cost you to believe: relationships, reputation, etc.? What were you afraid to let go of? What helped you let go of those fears?
- In your words, why is the Gospel worth living for and dying for?

> Jesus didn't die to save you from Hell. He died to save you from sin. And if He can't save you from sin, He can't save you from Hell.
>
> ADRIAN ROGERS

DAY 6

ETERNAL SECURITY: A SCRIPTURAL DEFENSE

PRACTICE IT

Though we studied several Scriptures about eternal security and clarified their meaning, there are several more that can confuse people. It is always important to study the context of Scripture to accurately understand what the author intended to say. Through the passages we read this week, we can be certain that if we are in Christ, we are eternally secure. Though we might struggle and stumble in sin, we endure until the end.

If you are a child of God, you can know that you are saved forever and rejoice. Rest in His love and, out of gratitude, serve Him with your life. If you are not saved, you can be right now. Jesus lived a perfect life, sacrificed Himself in death, and won your eternal victory in His resurrection. He made a way for you to live in Heaven with Him forever. If you would like to accept salvation, pray and accept His gracious, free gift. Put your faith in Him and come under His Lordship. Then thank Him because the work He has done in your heart is eternal and you are eternally secure.

PROCLAIM IT

Hopefully you wrote down some of the important elements of your personal spiritual journey in receiving the Gospel. Write down the story of your salvation and ask God to give you the courage and opportunity to share it with someone else. Sharing your testimony with others is powerful.

If you prayed to receive Christ, please share your decision with another Christian you know or with your pastor. We would also like to hear about it, so that we can provide you with free resources to help you grow in your new faith. Please let us know by going to **lwf.org/discover-jesus**, scrolling down the page and clicking on *I Believe*.

> On the permanence of your salvation: God will clean house, but He won't move out.
>
> ADRIAN ROGERS

> Spirit-dependence gives us the power to resist every temptation.
>
> ADRIAN ROGERS

WEEK 5

HOW CAN I LIVE A SPIRIT-FILLED LIFE?

INTRODUCTION

A man bought his very first car but didn't know anything about the mechanics of operating a vehicle. He loved the way it looked, and he showed it to all his friends with excitement and joy. However, every time he took it for a ride, he manually pushed it up every hill and jumped in the driver's seat to coast as it rolled all the way down. He didn't even know there was an engine, so he never turned it on! Rather than the car being a blessing, it was a burden because he operated it by his own strength. This made up story is an illustration that describes a Christian who doesn't understand the ministry of the Holy Spirit.

When God saved you, He gave you faith with an engine in it. Many people push their faith rather than letting their faith carry them. Salvation is a blessing, not a burden. If we want to be effective Christians, we need to understand how to turn the ignition and depend on the Holy Spirit. This week, we will study Ephesians 5 to discover how we can live by the Spirit.

PRAY OVER IT

> Dear God, Thank you for the gift of the Holy Spirit to all who believe! I confess that sometimes I don't live as if that is true, and sometimes I fail to obey. I know that I can depend on Him to aid me through all of life's challenges. Help me to understand what it means to live a Spirit-filled life so that Jesus can be exalted in my life. In Jesus' Name, Amen.

DAY 1

THE OBEDIENCE OF THE SPIRIT-FILLED CHRISTIAN

▨ PONDER IT

Every Christian is commanded to be Spirit-filled. It is not merely a suggestion. Paul wrote "be filled," not "get filled." It isn't a one-time occurrence, but a constant state of being.

And do not be drunk with wine, in which is dissipation; but be filled with the Spirit (Ephesians 5:18).

Though we are given the Holy Spirit when we are saved, we make the decision moment by moment to follow His lead. Being filled with the Holy Spirit means living by what *He* does in and through you, not by what *you* do.

Often, we focus more on the part of the verse that talks about drinking. But Paul is saying that being filled with the Holy Spirit is even more important than not being drunk. The Bible teaches that the sins of omission are greater than the sins of commission. It is a greater sin to fail to do what is commanded of you than to do what you should not do. Ultimately, if you do what is commanded of you, you will not do the things you shouldn't. Spirit-dependence gives us the power to resist every temptation, including drunkenness.

PUT IT IN WRITING

- When someone is drunk, what is controlling their actions? When you are filled with the Spirit, what is controlling your actions?
- What does it look like to be spirit-filled? How do you know that the Holy Spirit is working in and through you?

The Holy Spirit never
leaves a surrendered vessel
unfilled or unused.

ADRIAN ROGERS

DAY 2

A SPIRIT-FILLED WORSHIP LIFE AND MARRIAGE

PONDER IT

God gave Christians many commands in the Bible, but it is impossible for us to follow them in our own strength. It is only by the strength of the Holy Spirit that we are able to do what God has commanded of us. All aspects of our lives are to be filled with the Holy Spirit.

Worship life—God is spirit, and Christians must worship Him in spirit and in truth.

> **...speaking to one another in psalms and hymns and spiritual songs, singing and making melody in your heart to the Lord, giving thanks always for all things to God the Father in the name of our Lord Jesus Christ (Ephesians 5:19-20).**

When we are Spirit-filled, we are filled with blessings and joy as we worship Him. You can feel a tangible difference between worshiping Him in the flesh and worshiping Him in spirit.

Marriage—It is our human nature to live by our own will, standing up for our own preferences and desires, so God's commands to husbands and wives are equally difficult and impossible without the power of the Holy Spirit.

> **Wives, submit to your own husbands, as to the Lord. For the husband is head of the wife, as also Christ is head of the church; and He is the Savior of the body (Ephesians 5:22-23).**

In today's culture, it is unpopular to believe that wives are to submit to their husbands, but God commanded it in Christian marriages. Though man and woman are equal in God's sight (see Galatians 3:28), He has intentionally given husband and wife separate roles in the home so that families can function properly. However, when a woman lives by the Spirit, God gives her the strength to submit to her husband, even when it's difficult. When wives submit begrudgingly to their husbands, they are carrying out the command by their own effort. But when the Holy Spirit gives a woman the power to submit, she can do it joyfully while trusting God fully.

But husbands are also given a difficult command: to treat their wives with great devotion and self-sacrifice.

Husbands, love your wives, just as Christ also loved the church and gave Himself for her (Ephesians 5:25).

Christ loved the Church sacrificially. He dedicated His life to, and ultimately died for, the Church. A husband should love his wife so much that he is willing to die for her, and he proves it by the way he lives for her. A husband who loves his wife in this way, even when it's difficult, does so in the power of the Holy Spirit.

The only way we can love like Jesus is if He is inside us. If you are married, you must love your spouse as God has commanded you to. Physical attraction and chemistry can change, but God's Spirit inside us remains the same. Loving your spouse by following the commands of Ephesians 5 is only possible when we live by the Spirit.

PUT IT IN WRITING

- How would you describe your worship? Do you invite the Holy Spirit into your worship life? Do you worship in spirit and in truth?
- Is your marriage spirit-filled? In what ways do you need the Holy Spirit to help you love your spouse and fulfill the difficult commands of Ephesians 5? How do you know when you are obeying in your own strength or in the strength of the Holy Spirit?

> I can preach truth, but only the
> Holy Spirit can impart truth.
>
> ADRIAN ROGERS

DAY 3

SPIRIT-FILLLED WORK ETHIC, WARFARE, AND CHRISTIAN WITNESS

PONDER IT

Yesterday we considered what a Spirit-filled worship life and marriage would look like. Today we are going to consider how the Holy Spirit should impact three more areas of our lives.

Work ethic—If we are to represent Christ and live in righteousness, our work ethic must also be fueled by the Spirit. You are to serve your boss as if he were Jesus Christ.

> **Bondservants, be obedient to those who are your masters according to the flesh, with fear and trembling, in sincerity of heart, as to Christ (Ephesians 6:5).**

This is difficult to do, especially when we serve unkind and incompetent leaders. But with the power of the Holy Spirit, we are called to obey those in authority over us.

Spiritual warfare—We have a sinister, malevolent enemy: the devil. He is active, and he wants to take every Christian down.

> **Finally, my brethren, be strong in the Lord and in the power of His might. Put on the whole armor of God, that you may be able to stand against the wiles of the devil (Ephesians 6:10-11).**

Without God, Satan is stronger than our spirit. But when we are dependent on the Holy Spirit, we have a greater power inside of us (see 1 John 4:4).

Witness—Our evangelism is in vain unless the Spirit of God is in it.

> ...praying always with all prayer and supplication in the Spirit, being watchful to this end with all perseverance and supplication for all the saints—and for me, that utterance may be given to me, that I may open my mouth boldly to make known the mystery of the gospel (Ephesians 6:18-19).

Whether we witness on the street, in the marketplace, in the classroom, in the home, or from the pulpit, our words are empty unless they are spoken from the Spirit. Only He has the power to grip the heart of the unsaved man.

When we live by the Spirit in our obedience and obligations, we do not miss heavenly opportunities. We are to look around and watch for opportunities to share the Gospel. It is imperative that we share Christ with our hurting world. People are more hungry for the Gospel and more open to Jesus than ever before. As the night grows darker, the saints grow brighter. We must be Spirit-filled believers so we do not let opportunities to witness pass us by.

The Church fulfills the will of God when we share Christ. When we make disciples, those people go and make more disciples. It takes every Christian living by the Spirit to fulfill the Great Commission.

PUT IT IN WRITING

- How can you become more Spirit-dependent in your workplace or in the community you serve? How would it affect your professional relationships to depend on the power of the Holy Spirit?
- Are you fighting a spiritual battle in your own strength or depending on the strength of the Spirit? How do you know the difference?
- What role does the Holy Spirit play in evangelism? What opportunities is God giving you to be a witness for Him?

> It takes every Christian living by the Spirit to fulfill the Great Commission.
>
> ADRIAN ROGERS

DAY 4

THE REQUIREMENTS OF THE SPIRIT-FILLED CHRISTIAN

PONDER IT

It is important to remember that the Holy Spirit is not a substance or object; He is a person. He is the living, active Spirit of God who enables us to do everything that the Lord requires of us.

We are vessels, and He dwells inside of us, giving us the power to do good works. We are His temple.

> **Or do you not know that your body is the temple of the Holy Spirit who is in you, whom you have from God, and you are not your own (1 Corinthians 6:19)?**

You must be completely committed to the Holy Spirit. Welcome Him into your heart, mind, and body. Allow Him to use all of you, not just one part. Give Him access to your social life, your business affairs, your dating relationship or marriage, your financial security, and every other area of your life. This is true commitment.

You must allow the Holy Spirit continual control over your life. You must give over control to Him every moment of every day.

Drunkards use wine to relinquish control of their bodies and let go. As Christians, rather than giving control of ourselves to something sinful, we must relinquish control of our thoughts, emotions, desires, and choices to the Holy Spirit. It is the wisest decision we could possibly make, and it is what God commands of us.

On the day of Pentecost, the apostles were accused of being drunk with wine (Acts 2:15). They were not drunk with wine, but with the Holy Spirit. When a person is drunk with alcohol, everything about him changes: his speech slurs, his body language is clumsy, and his decisions are poor. When a man is controlled by the Holy Spirit, his entire being also changes, but those changes reflect holiness and glorify God. The one thing that being drunk with wine and being drunk with the Holy Spirit have in common is that the person being controlled always wants more. When we allow the Holy Spirit to control our lives, we keep coming back for more! God gladly gives us more; in fact, He wants us to hunger for more.

You must claim the fullness of a Spirit-filled life. Just as you received the Lord Jesus by faith, you walk by faith every day. We do this by continually remembering that His Holy Spirit fills us. Claim the truth that His power is in you, enabling you to live a wholehearted life in Christ.

PUT IT IN WRITING

- Is there an area of your life you have not fully committed to the Holy Spirit? What does it look like for you to give Him complete and continual control over your life?
- In what ways do you need to claim the fullness of a Spirit-filled life? What would it look like for you to embrace the reality that His power is within you?

I don't look for a feeling; I claim the filling.

ADRIAN ROGERS

DAY 5

THE RESULTS OF A SPIRIT-FILLED LIFE

PONDER IT

When we understand the reasons for, and the requirements of, a Spirit-filled life, and dedicate ourselves to rely wholly on Him, we will see tangible results. We will see evidence of His work in our lives. You can have assurance that you are living a Spirit-filled life when you see these results in your life:

You will have more adoration for God. When you desire to worship God, telling Him about your love for Him, you are Spirit-filled. You cannot help but sing to Him in praise and adoration. Your life will overflow with affection toward God.

> **...speaking to one another in psalms and hymns and spiritual songs, singing and making melody in your heart to the Lord (Ephesians 5:19).**

You will have a spirit of appreciation. A Spirit-filled person is humbly grateful, but a flesh-filled person is grumbly hateful. When you are filled with the Holy Spirit, you constantly thank God for His work in your heart and life.

> **...giving thanks always for all things to God the Father in the name of our Lord Jesus Christ (Ephesians 5:20).**

Paul didn't say to give thanks for *some* things, but for *all* things. Spirit-filled Christians see God's providence in their lives, even when life is difficult. You are marked with the Spirit when you overflow with unconditional, heavenly gratitude.

You will have a spirit of accommodation. Submission is not just for wives; it is for all Christians.

> **...submitting to one another in fear of God (Ephesians 5:21).**

The word "submitting" in this verse is the same Greek word that Peter used when he told servants to submit to their masters (see 1 Peter 2:18). We are to count ourselves lower than others, just as a servant is lower than his master. We must devote ourselves to one another in humility and service, regardless of how others respond to us.

If you are a believer and you see a gap between where you are and where you want to be, take a minute to check your motives. Many times we want to be filled with the Holy Spirit for the wrong reasons. Your proud self wants to be filled with the Holy Spirit to be a superior Christian, the best one you know. Your lazy self believes that if you're filled with the Holy Spirit, you can coast along through life and don't have to put forth any effort. Your ambitious self says that if you're filled with the Holy Spirit you'll be a great Bible teacher, a great singer, a great preacher, or a great evangelist.

But God is not interested in those motivations. The Holy Spirit's single ministry is to exalt the Lord Jesus Christ. When the burning ambition of your heart is to exalt the Lord Jesus and you give him the key to every room, then you are filled with the Holy Spirit.

PUT IT IN WRITING

- What are the qualities of God that you most adore? Do you feel like you are adoring Him more than you have before? Why or why not?
- What are the things you are most grateful for right now? What are the difficult circumstances you are grateful for?
- What does it mean for you to accommodate or submit to others in your earthly relationships?

> True worship is all that I am responding to all that He is in gratitude and praise.
>
> ADRIAN ROGERS

DAY 6

HOW TO HAVE A SPIRIT-FILLED LIFE

PRACTICE IT

The fullness of the Spirit is only available to those who are under the control of the Spirit and submitted to His purpose. Live by faith and be filled with the Spirit. No matter what happens in your life, respond to Him in praise, adoration, and gratitude. Let your life be marked with service to others and fear of the Lord. Then, you will know you are living a Spirit-filled life.

Ask yourself: Am I filled with the Spirit of God right now? If you are not committed to Him, handing over to Him full control of your life, and claiming the promise of His Spirit, the answer is "no." If you are a Christian, the Spirit is inside of you, whether or not you live as if that is true. Pray, asking the Holy Spirit to help you depend on Him and live by His guidance.

If you are not saved, you can invite Christ into your heart and receive the Holy Spirit today. Pray, believing in the sinless life, the sacrificial death, and the victorious resurrection of Christ. Submit yourself to Jesus as Lord. Then, thank Him for sending His Holy Spirit to empower you to live for Him. Receive the power of the Holy Spirit and rejoice in gratitude that you are a new creation in Christ!

PROCLAIM IT

Spend some quiet time this week in prayer, inviting the Holy Spirit to come into your life more completely and more fully. Clear the distractions so that you can hear His voice. Share with a trusted friend or mentor what you feel like He said to you, and then be willing to walk in obedience to what He is calling you to believe or do.

If you prayed to receive Christ, please share your decision with another Christian you know or with your pastor. We would also like to hear about it, so that we can provide you with free resources to help you grow in your new faith. Please let us know by going to **lwf.org/discover-jesus**, scrolling down the page and clicking on I *Believe*.

> Being saved is not a matter of what you do for God, but it is a matter of what God does through you by the fullness of the Holy Spirit.
>
> ADRIAN ROGERS

> God is not interested so much in making you happy and healthy as He is in making you holy.
>
> ADRIAN ROGERS

WEEK 6

HOW CAN I TURN TEMPTATIONS INTO TRIUMPHS?

INTRODUCTION

Many of us think that only bad comes from temptation, but we can actually use temptation to grow in the grace and knowledge of Christ.

> **Therefore let him who thinks he stands take heed lest he fall. No temptation has overtaken you except such as is common to man; but God is faithful, who will not allow you to be tempted beyond what you are able, but with the temptation will also make the way of escape, that you may be able to bear it. Therefore, my beloved, flee from idolatry (1 Corinthians 10:12-14).**

In general, we deal with temptation in three ways. Some people simply give in to it. They believe that if it feels good, it must be okay. They make an idol of self-gratification. Others spend all of their time fighting temptation, but they do it in the strength of the flesh. They fight on their own and they fail.

But the third way to tackle temptation is to overcome it through the power of Christ. In Christ, our temptations become triumphs. This week, we will study 1 Corinthians 10 to learn how to triumph over temptation.

PRAY OVER IT

> *Dear God, I confess that I sometimes feel powerless to resist sin. But Your Word says I can overcome temptation through the power of Your Spirit. Help me to see more clearly where I am being tempted, and to learn how to rely on Your strength so that my temptations can become triumphs. In Jesus' Name, Amen.*

DAY 1

THE SUBJECTS OF TEMPTATION

PONDER IT

All of us are subject to temptation. Even Jesus was tempted in the wilderness. In fact, Satan loves to make those in Christian ministry and leadership his biggest targets. We are all faced with the temptations of pride, materialism, dishonesty, greed, and lust. Being saved does not make us immune to temptation. In fact, when we think we can't be tempted, we become even more vulnerable.

> **Therefore let him who thinks he stands take heed lest he fall (1 Corinthians 10:12).**

Though temptation is not desirable, it is not a sin to be tempted. We know that because Jesus was without sin (see Hebrews 4:15). However, 1 Corinthians 10:12 warns against pride because the proud man tempts the devil to tempt him. If you think that you cannot fall or can handle temptation in your own strength, you are headed for a fall.

You might wonder why God allows us to be tempted. If God really loves us, why doesn't God just kill the devil? If He did, we would lose the opportunity and ability to become overcomers through the Lord Jesus Christ. We would also lose the ability to make choices.

Without opposition, there is no victory. God has not called you to a life of ease, but He has called you to a life of victory through our Lord Jesus Christ.

PUT IT IN WRITING

- Do you consider yourself unable to be tempted? Why or why not?
- What temptations are you currently facing? Where are you facing opposition from the devil? In what way are your temptations opportunities for victory?

> The Bible does not say, "Don't walk in the flesh and you will fulfill the desires of the Spirit. Rather, it says, "Walk in the Spirit and you won't fulfill the desires of the flesh.
>
> ADRIAN ROGERS

DAY 2

THE SOURCE OF TEMPTATION

■ PONDER IT

Everyone faces temptation, and if we want to withstand it, we need to know where it comes from.

> **No temptation has overtaken you except such as is common to man (1 Corinthians 10:13a).**

You may think that you struggle with a temptation that is unique to you, but that is a lie. Three sources of temptation are common to everyone: the world, the flesh, and the devil. Those sources of temptation affect our spirits, souls, and bodies.

> **...and may your whole spirit, soul, and body be preserved blameless at the coming of our Lord Jesus Christ (1 Thessalonians 5:23b).**

The world—The world doesn't tempt us through the good parts of creation. We are created to love people and nature, and God declared these things good. The material world is not inherently bad. But when the Bible talks about "the world," it refers to the *things* or *order* of the world, which is systematized evil.

> **Do not love the world or the things in the world. If anyone loves the world, the love of the Father is not in him (1 John 2:15).**

> **And do not be conformed to this world, but be transformed by the renewing of your mind (Romans 12:2a).**

> **Adulterers and adulteresses! Do you not know that friendship with the world is enmity with God? Whoever therefore wants to be a friend of the world makes himself an enemy of God (James 4:4).**

We can all fall into ordering our lives in the way of the world. We can become obsessed with sports, business, politics, and anything else. These things aren't inherently wrong, but when we let something other than Jesus be our Lord, the world becomes our kingdom rather than the kingdom of God. The orders and systems of the world are an external foe to the soul.

The flesh—The Bible talks about the flesh as a source of temptation—not in a literal sense, meaning your skin and bones—but in terms of our sin nature.

> **For the flesh lusts against the Spirit, and the Spirit against the flesh; and these are contrary to one another, so that you do not do the things that you wish (Galatians 5:17).**

We all have an inherited predisposition to sin. The devil doesn't force you to sin. Sin is an inside job, and it comes from your flesh, your sin nature. The devil uses your flesh to tempt you, but you are the one who ultimately chooses to sin.

The devil—The third source of temptation is the devil. He will work hard to get you to sin, and he will use the world and the flesh to do it. He is real, he is active, and you must resist him.

> **Be sober, be vigilant; because your adversary the devil walks about like a roaring lion, seeking whom he may devour. Resist him, steadfast in the faith, knowing that the same sufferings are experienced by your brotherhood in the world (1 Peter 5:8-9).**

PUT IT IN WRITING

- How does it impact you to know that temptation is common to all people? What does it mean to know that you are not the only one who struggles?
- When you consider the temptation you are currently facing, is it a temptation of the world, the flesh or the devil? What kinds of temptations do you see coming from these three sources?

DAY 3

THE TARGET OF TEMPTATION

▪ PONDER IT

Temptation comes from different sources, but it affects three primary parts of us: spirit, soul, and body.

...and may your whole spirit, soul, and body be preserved blameless at the coming of our Lord Jesus Christ (1 Thessalonians 5:23b).

Because you are made in the image of the triune God, you have three distinct parts: soul, spirit, and body. You are one individual with three parts, and you can be tempted in each of them. You need to understand them, so you understand how to fight your temptations.

Soul—The soul is your mind, emotions, and will. The world, the external foe, will primarily tempt you in your soul. It will tempt your mind and try to corrupt your ego. It will play on your emotions to try to get your will to choose sin.

In Genesis 13, Abram (later called Abraham by God) and his nephew Lot had a disagreement. Abram decided to let Lot pick his land, and Abram would take the other piece of land. Lot chose the land that was lush and good for his cattle, even though he already had plenty of well-fed livestock. He wasn't hungry or in need of anything. Though he was already fabulously wealthy, he wanted to do more, be more, and have more. He wanted to feed his ego by becoming the greatest rancher in all of Palestine. He fed his soul on the things of the world.

Many of us today are tempted exactly that way. The world says that we need to do more, be more, and have more. This is the lust of the eyes, the lust of the flesh, and the pride of life. It's not of our heavenly Father; it's of the world and wars against the soul.

Body—The flesh is not the same as the body. The flesh, our predisposition to sin, wars against the body. We face physical temptations in the areas of appetite, lust, laziness, and violence. The flesh uses the needs of the body as a vehicle of sin. All people—young and old, male and female—struggle in this area.

The Bible has many examples of this kind of temptation. King David struggled with physical lust. In 2 Samuel 11-12, he saw Bathsheba, a beautiful woman, bathing on her roof. He watched her and he wanted to have her. His sexual temptation overcame him. His sexual drive and physical emotions, both given by God, succumbed to temptation of the flesh. He sinned, committing adultery with Bathsheba and meeting those needs in a sinful way. His passions and physical frame were under attack.

The external foe (the world) wars against the soul. Like Lot, we face the temptation to protect our ego and pride. The internal foe (the flesh) wars against the body. Like David, we are tempted to commit physical acts of sin.

PUT IT IN WRITING

- What in your life do you see tempting your soul? In what ways are you tempted to follow the ways of the world and participate in its systems and structures?
- What in your life is tempting your body? Which physical area do you struggle with: appetite, lust, laziness, violence? How would you explain the difference between a God-given desire and a sinful desire?

> The things of this world will never satisfy the longings of your heart. A round world cannot fit into a three-cornered heart.
>
> ADRIAN ROGERS

DAY 4

THE INFERNAL FOE

PONDER IT

We have an internal foe, an external foe, and an infernal foe: the devil. Satan primarily wars against your spirit.

The difference between your soul and your spirit is this: your soul is the sense of self-consciousness, and your spirit is the sense of God-consciousness. You know God through your spirit. A plant has a body but not a soul. An animal has a body and a soul, which is self-consciousness, but not a spirit. Only a man has a spirit, which is what makes a man greater than an animal.

You can know God because God's spirit bears witness with your spirit that you are a child of God. The Bible says that God is spirit, and we must worship him in spirit and in truth (see John 4:24). Your spirit is the vehicle of communication with God, worship, praise, and spiritual knowledge. The devil, the infernal foe, wants to cut you off from God, so he wars against your spirit.

Satan is a crafty foe. You might think that all he wants is for you to lose everything and be humiliated. But that is not necessarily true. If you were a drunkard covered in flies and vomit, you wouldn't be good advertising for the devil. He would rather give you a crisp, white collar, surround you with beautiful women and handsome men, and give you a life that seems desirable, but godless. He will give you intelligence, money, comfort, manners, pleasure, and popularity, so long as you stay far from the Lord. The devil gives us a taste of earthly success so that we will rely on ourselves rather than on God.

The world tempted Lot's soul with the inflation of his ego through wealth. The flesh tempted David's body in the sexual lusts of his flesh. But the devil tempted Simon Peter's spirit by leading him to think that escaping earthly persecution was more important than representing Jesus. Jesus told Simon Peter that he would betray Him three times.

"Simon, Simon! Indeed, Satan has asked for you, that he may sift you as wheat. But I have prayed for you, that your faith should not fail; and when you have returned to Me, strengthen your brethren" (Luke 22:31-32).

When Peter denied Christ, it wasn't his flesh or his ego that was under attack; it was his faith. Jesus prayed that Peter's faith would be strengthened. The devil wanted him to fear what men would say or do to him more than he cared about standing up for Christ. Satan tried to separate Peter from Almighty God, and that is what he wants for you. The devil tempts your spirit by attacking your faith.

PUT IT IN WRITING

- Can you name an instance when the devil tempted your spirit? How did you respond and what was the outcome?
- What kind of temptation do you think is the most dangerous? Why? Which temptation do you find yourself battling the most?

> God will test us, but God will not tempt us. God tests us to make us stand. Satan tempts us to make us fall.
>
> ADRIAN ROGERS

DAY 5

FLIGHT, FAITH, AND FIGHT

PONDER IT

We know that we can be tempted in soul, body, and flesh. But the big question is this: How do we overcome temptation?

> **...but God is faithful, who will not allow you to be tempted beyond what you are able, but with the temptation will also make the way of escape (1 Corinthians 10:13b).**

Bible teacher Donald Grey Barnhouse preached about three concepts that help us resist temptation: flight, faith, and fight.

FLIGHT

> **Flee also youthful lusts; but pursue righteousness, faith, love, peace with those who call on the Lord out of a pure heart (2 Timothy 2:22).**

We must flee the lusts of the flesh. Because we are not built to fight these temptations, we are told to flee. When you are faced with temptation of the flesh, you must avoid situations that cause you to stumble. When you don't flee temptation, it is like playing with a match in dry grass.

If you want to be pure, you must do everything you can to remove yourself from fleshly temptation. If abusing alcohol is a temptation, do not bring it into your home. If you are trying to quit smoking, don't keep an extra pack stashed away. If you are tempted by sexual sin, never be alone with the object of your lust.

FAITH

> **For whatever is born of God overcomes the world. And this is the victory that has overcome the world—our faith (1 John 5:4).**

We are not told to fight worldliness but to overcome it with faith. Faith makes God a bright, living reality to us. When we love the world, the love of the Father is not in us (see 1 John 2:15). But the opposite is also true—when we love the Father, our love of the world fades away. When you fill your mind and heart with holy things, the things of the world become less important.

FIGHT

Therefore submit to God. Resist the devil and he will flee from you (James 4:7).

Though we are not to fight the temptations of lust and the world, we are to fight the devil. We are not told to run from him but to fight and resist him. But we do not fight by our own strength but by the Holy Spirit's strength in us.

You cannot live passively, expecting Satan to leave you alone. It is not a matter of *if* he will tempt you, but *when*. You must be ready to resist him in the name of Jesus (see Revelation 12:11). The devil is not afraid of your resolutions, intentions, or good will. He fears the cleansing blood of Christ. When Satan comes against you, bring the Word of God against him.

Be strong in the Lord and in the power of His might. Satan does not want you to understand the power that you have to overcome temptation. But you can always overcome temptation if you remember these words: flight, faith, and fight.

PUT IT IN WRITING

- When you consider the temptations you are facing, what does it look like for you to flee, have faith, and fight the devil?
- How has God helped you overcome temptation in the past?

> When temptation comes to you, don't be on the defensive—be on the offensive.
>
> ADRIAN ROGERS

DAY 6

HOW TO TURN TEMPTATIONS INTO TRIUMPHS

▪ PRACTICE IT

We are not promised a life without temptation. In fact, temptations are guaranteed to us before we get to Heaven. But by God's power, we can have the strength to overcome the attacks of the flesh, the world, and the devil.

If you have not yet accepted Christ as your Lord and Savior, you cannot ultimately overcome temptation. We do not have the power to overcome the temptation to sin on our own. But there is great news: when you are saved, the Holy Spirit comes to dwell inside of you. This Spirit of God gives us the power to overcome and resist temptations of all kinds so that we can live lives of wholeness that please God.

If you would like to be saved, you can be, right now. Pray, trusting in the life, death, and resurrection of Christ, which has paid for your sin-debt. Acknowledge Jesus as Lord. Then thank Him, accepting the new life that you have in Him as your Lord and Savior.

PROCLAIM IT

If you are struggling with the temptation of a particular sin, talk to a trusted Christian friend or mentor about it. Be specific. The devil wants us to minimize our sin and hide it. Instead, ask your friend to hold you accountable and pray for the strength and wisdom to overcome sin. Determine if the temptation is of your soul, body, or spirit, and respond accordingly by strengthening the part of you that is being attacked.

If you prayed to receive Christ, please share your decision with another Christian you know or with your pastor. We would also like to hear about it, so that we can provide you with free resources to help you grow in your new faith. Please let us know by going to **lwf.org/discover-jesus**, scrolling down the page and clicking on *I Believe*.

> If the devil never bothers you, it's because you're both going in the same direction.
>
> ADRIAN ROGERS

> The Holy Spirit of God convicts Christians of sin. It shows up as a headache, an inability to concentrate, a stomach ache, an inability to pray, and in many other ways.
>
> ADRIAN ROGERS

WEEK 7

HOW DO I DEAL WITH SIN IN MY LIFE?

INTRODUCTION

One of Satan's greatest strategies is to tell us that we can sin and get away with it. He uses this lie to try to take down even the strongest Christians. If we fall into sin, Satan then shifts from the tempter into the accuser. He leads us to discouragement. He wants us to believe that we are so out of balance that God would never accept us again.

In the Old Testament, Satan used these classic lies when he tempted King David to commit adultery with Bathsheba, and then to cover it up by killing her husband, Uriah. After David committed these sins and was called out by Nathan, he was in the pit of despair. In his remorse, he cried out to the Lord and wrote Psalm 51, a psalm of repentance.

David was not only a great sinner, but also a great repenter. Even though he sinned terribly, we can learn a lot from David. Even after this woeful season of his life, the Bible still called David "a man after God's own heart." David didn't let sin keep him away from making things right with God. This week, we will learn from David's example how to come back when we are down.

PRAY OVER IT

Dear God, You know that I struggle with sin, and my sin is not hidden from You. Thank you for loving me and for making a way for me to come back to You. Help me to see my sin more clearly and to repent of it more sincerely. I love You with all my heart, and I want to walk in Your ways. In Jesus' Name, Amen.

DAY 1

THE CAPABILITY OF SIN IN THE SAINT

▣ PONDER IT

We all have the capability to sin. When we get saved, we don't lose our capacity to sin. Many times our sin sprouts from an unexpected opportunity and an undetected weakness. When those two come together, we fall into sin.

> **If we say that we have no sin, we deceive ourselves, and the truth is not in us (1 John 1:8).**

Once we are saved, our sin cannot take away our salvation. But that does not mean that we can sin with impunity. If you put your hand on a hot stove, you get burned. If you're bound to sin, you're bound to suffer. Each of us has specific temptations and tendencies that we struggle with. If indulged, these sins lead us to darkness, depression, and death.

The eternal security of the believer is not a license to sin. If we live in sin, we reject a life of wholeness and light that is offered by the Gospel. When we give into sin, we face the consequences listed in Psalm 51.

> **Have mercy upon me, O God, according to Your lovingkindness; according to the multitude of Your tender mercies, blot out my transgressions. Wash me thoroughly from my iniquity, and cleanse me from my sin (Psalm 51:1-2).**

Sin soils our soil. David asked God to wash and cleanse him from his sin. He felt filthy in his heart.

One way that you can know that you are saved is if you feel dirty when you sin. When a child of the devil sins, he or she feels no remorse. But when a child of God sins, it bothers him or her. A pig never feels dirty in the mud because that is its natural habitat. But when a sheep falls into the mud, it wants to get out. When you have the Holy Spirit inside you, there is no rest when you are living in sin. The discomfort of living out of fellowship with God causes us to feel like fish out of water.

Sin saturates the mind. What David had done reverberated through his soul and echoed through his conscience.

For I acknowledge my transgressions, and my sin is always before me (Psalm 51:3).

If you can sin and easily forget it, you likely are not saved. When you are saved, the Holy Spirit of God convicts Christians of sin. It shows up as a headache, an inability to concentrate, a stomach ache, an inability to pray, and in many other ways. The reminder of sin doesn't escape the believer's mind, but an unsaved person carries on in his folly.

PUT IT IN WRITING

- Think of a time you fell into sin. What parts of Psalm 51:1-3 resonate with how you felt?
- When you are convicted of sin, how does the Holy Spirit usually make you aware of it? What types of discomfort have you experienced?

> ## If you can sin and easily forget it, you likely are not saved.
>
> ADRIAN ROGERS

DAY 2

SIN STINGS THE CONSCIENCE

PONDER IT

Two kinds of wounds come to the human psyche: sorrow and guilt. Sorrow is a clean wound that will heal in time. We experience sorrow through grief over death and other painful things we cannot control. But guilt is a dirty wound that festers until it is cleansed. Guilt comes from sin.

Sin stings the conscience. In this verse, David didn't cry out against the punisher, but against his sin. He wasn't just bothered by the consequences of his sin, but by hurting his Heavenly Father's heart. David saw sin for what it really is, an affront to a Holy God—the God who loved him, the God who had redeemed him.

> **Against You, You only, have I sinned, and done this evil in Your sight (Psalm 51:4a).**

If the only thing you fear when you sin is the punishment, then you are not saved. If you're a child of God who sins, you don't weep primarily because you're going to get punished. You weep primarily because you have disgraced your God. That is the difference between a slave and a son. A slave, when he disobeys, fears his master's whip. But when a loving son disobeys, he aches over the father's displeasure. He is brokenhearted that he has broken the heart of God.

PUT IT IN WRITING

- When have you experienced sorrow and guilt over your sin?
- Do you relate more to the slave or to the loving son? In what way?

Sin is not just breaking God's laws; it is breaking His heart.

ADRIAN ROGERS

DAY 3

SIN SADDENS THE HEART AND SICKENS THE BODY

PONDER IT

Sin saddens the heart. Notice that David didn't ask that his salvation would be restored, but that the *joy* of his salvation would return.

> **Make me hear joy and gladness, that the bones You have broken may rejoice. ...Restore to me the joy of Your salvation, and uphold me by Your generous Spirit (Psalm 51:8, 12).**

You can be saved and be miserable. The most miserable man on Earth is not an unsaved man, but a saved man out of fellowship with God. Many unsaved people are having a ball, relishing in the temporary pleasures of sin. But the joy of a saved man who is living in fellowship with God is unmatched. When we sin, we lose the immense joy of that fellowship, and David wanted it to be restored.

A test of your salvation is this: Do you have unspeakable joy in your heart? Though believers can experience unhappiness, they can never lose their joyful response to God's glory. It is a fruit of the Spirit that doesn't waiver through life's circumstances. No earthly hardship can take your joy because earthly sources didn't give it to you in the first place. We lose our joy when we do not abide in Jesus. Jesus gives us joy; it is joy in the Lord. Joy doesn't help you remove pain, but it does help you endure it.

Sin sickens the body. God did not literally break David's bones. David is using poetry, as if someone today were to say, "I am crushed." God had him under extreme pressure and he felt it in his body.

> **Make me hear joy and gladness, that the bones You have broken may rejoice (Psalm 51:8).**

When we sin, God puts us in a state of discomfort and unrest. For David, it was as if God was squeezing the life out of him. If you keep that pressure on for a long time, it will make you sick. One of the reasons for sickness is sin in the life of a child of God. Paul talked about sin in this way:

For this reason many are weak and sick among you, and many sleep (1 Corinthians 11:30).

Unrepentant sin will make you sick, sometimes even unto death. On the contrary, when you are right with God, you stand straighter, smile more, digest food better, and sleep better. The Bible says that a merry heart is good medicine (see Proverbs 17:22). But you can't have the joy of the Lord if you are walking away from God. David was a child of God, and when he walked in sin, he was miserable.

PUT IT IN WRITING

- Explain why being sad over your sin is a sign that you are saved. Has your heart ever been saddened by sin? Has your sin ever affected your physical health? What restored your joy?
- What is the joy of the Lord? What has that looked like in your life?

> The most miserable man on Earth is not an unsaved man, but a saved man out of fellowship with God.
>
> ADRIAN ROGERS

DAY 4

SIN SOURS THE SPIRIT AND SEALS OUR LIPS

PONDER IT

Sin sours the spirit. David had a sour and wrong spirit, and so do we when we walk away from God.

> **Create in me a clean heart, O God, and renew a steadfast spirit within me (Psalm 51:10).**

Christians who are dwelling in sin can be the most miserable people to be around because they are not at peace in their souls. They push their own internal misery off on everyone else. They are critical, negative, and short-fused; they have sour spirits.

David was the perfect example of this. He committed adultery with Bathsheba, and then, while trying to cover up his first sin, he committed murder. He ordered Bathsheba's husband, Uriah, into battle and ordered Uriah's comrades to abandon him so that Uriah was killed.

Nathan the prophet came to speak to David about his sin. He told David a story about a poor man who had a little lamb that was like his own daughter. It even ate at his table. Next door lived a rich man who had thousands of sheep. This rich man had a stranger stop by, so he went to the poor man's house, took his lamb, killed it, and fed it to the visitor. Nathan asked David what should be done to the rich man, since David was the king and made these decisions. David was filled with rage and said that the rich man should pay fourfold. Then, Nathan explained to him that it was an analogy, and David was actually the rich man who took something that didn't belong to him (see 2 Samuel 12).

Those who are living in sin are very quick to judge people for their sin, even though their own sin is greater. They try to pick specks of dust out of other people's eyes when they have logs in their own (see Matthew 7:1-5). If you have a sour spirit, the remedy is to get right with God.

Sin seals our lips. Sin in the life of a Christian ruins worship. David said that he couldn't worship or praise God because of his sin.

> **Deliver me from the guilt of bloodshed, O God, the God of my salvation, and my tongue shall sing aloud of Your righteousness. O Lord, open my lips, and my mouth shall show forth Your praise (Psalm 51:14-15).**

When people are living in sin, they stop praising God. They might sing, but it doesn't come from the heart. They stop sharing about Jesus because they are not right with God. When we sin, we don't sing.

PUT IT IN WRITING

- Have you been excessively critical of someone in your life? If so, have you checked your own heart? Is sin causing you to have a sour spirit?
- Have you stopped worshiping and praising God? Why is this difficult when you are living in sin? What do you need to do or believe in order to be made right with God?

> Sometimes the ravages of sin preempt the blessings of God.
>
> ADRIAN ROGERS

DAY 5

HAVE CONFIDENCE, MAKE A CONFESSION, AND RECEIVE CLEANSING

PONDER IT

No Christian is perfect, and we have all reaped the consequences of sin at one time or another. But we need to know how to come back after we walk away. Psalm 51 also helps us know the way back to God.

Have confidence. You must have confidence that God still loves you. David was confident in God's mercy. He knew that God was capable of loving him, even through his sin.

> **Have mercy upon me, O God, according to Your lovingkindness; according to the multitude of Your tender mercies, blot out my transgressions (Psalm 51:1).**

The devil loves to point out your sin. He will tell you that God is finished with you and that there is no hope, but those things are lies. Nothing you can do will make God stop loving you. Few have committed sins as grievous as David's sins, and yet, even David knew that God would be merciful toward him. For where there is great sin, there is also great grace.

Make a confession. These are the words of David's confession:

> **For I acknowledge my transgressions, and my sin is always before me. Against You, You only, have I sinned, and done this evil in Your sight—that You may be found just when You speak, and blameless when You judge (Psalm 51:3-4).**

David's acknowledgement is not just an admission of sin, but a confession, an agreement with God that he had sinned. God will not accept an excuse or an alibi. David could have said it wasn't his fault or tried to blame someone else. But instead, he made an honest confession, taking full responsibility and expressing remorse for his sin. God forgave David. God will do the same for us.

If we confess our sins, He is faithful and just to forgive us our sins and to cleanse us from all unrighteousness (1 John 1:9).

Receive cleansing.

Wash me thoroughly from my iniquity, and cleanse me from my sin. ...Purge me with hyssop, and I shall be clean; wash me, and I shall be whiter than snow (Psalm 51:2, 7).

When David asked God to wash him and purge him, he was addressing the pollution and power of sin. When you confess, God literally purges you on the inside. When you come to Him in honest repentance, He removes your guilt and condemnation.

When God blots out our sin, He erases the record. It doesn't exist anymore, never to be brought up again. Don't let the devil bring up something God has forgotten.

We have the capability to sin, and we experience the consequences of sin. Thank God for cleansing us of sin.

PUT IT IN WRITING

- Which one of these steps in confession is the most difficult for you: having confidence that God still loves you, making an honest confession, or receiving cleansing and forgiveness? What truths do you need to remember?
- Is it easy for you to believe that when you repent of your sin, you are washed "whiter than snow?" Why or why not?

> When we try to cover it, God uncovers it.
> But when we uncover it, God covers it.
>
> ADRIAN ROGERS

DAY 6

HOW TO COME BACK WHEN YOU ARE DOWN

PRACTICE IT

Where Satan brings condemnation, God brings cleansing. Every Christian stumbles and falls into sin. We live in a fallen world, awaiting the fullness of glory that comes in Heaven. When we sin, we need to pay attention to the warning signs that we are not right with God. We must repent, turn away, and receive the precious washing of the blood of Jesus.

If you are struggling with sin, repent. The Holy Spirit will give you the strength to stop, but you can't change what you don't acknowledge as sin. When you do, the Lord's forgiveness will wash over you, removing your sin as far as the east is from the west. Cast your sins on Him and receive the joy that comes from fellowship with the Lord.

If you have yet to accept Jesus as your Lord and Savior, you can right now. Pray, inviting Jesus into your heart, repenting of your sin, and trust that His perfect life, the sacrifice of His death, and the victory of His resurrection have made you clean.

PROCLAIM IT

If you have walked away from God, you can turn around and come back. If you are struggling with sin, you don't have to struggle alone. Share with a trusted mentor or friend the sin you have been struggling with or hiding. Ask that person to pray for you and to keep you accountable. Receive the forgiveness that God freely offers and turn away from your sin.

If people you know are struggling with sin, pray for them. Ask God to give you an opportunity to share what God has taught you this week about confession and repentance. If they want to turn around and walk back to God, walk with them and support them.

If you prayed to receive Christ, please share your decision with another Christian you know or with your pastor. We would also like to hear about it, so that we can provide you with free resources to help you grow in your new faith. Please let us know by going to **lwf.org/discover-jesus**, scrolling down the page and clicking on *I Believe*.

> I have been saved from the penalty of sin.
> I am being saved from the power of sin.
> I will be saved from the possibility of sin.
>
> ADRIAN ROGERS

No matter what is happening in your life, know that God is waiting for you with open arms.

ADRIAN ROGERS

WEEK 8

HOW DO I RESTORE FELLOWSHIP WITH GOD?

INTRODUCTION

Every person has healthy fears. When we see spiders or snakes, we jump back or run away. When we feel that we are in danger, looking down over a big cliff, or avoiding an erratic driver in traffic, our bodies naturally respond by sending us warning signals, helping us to take appropriate action. But we don't react with the same urgency when the temptation to sin is lurking around us, even though it is just as dangerous as any physical threat we could encounter.

Any Christian can slip and fall into sin, but a true child of God should fear sin, and a true child of God, though he may slip and fall, has a desire for a quick recovery.

We must ask the questions: What happens when I slip? How do I recover? How do I restore fellowship with Christ when I fail?

The Apostle John explained the answers in the Bible. He gave us the formula for fellowship, both with God and with other Christians. In order to have a cleansed life, we must deal with our sin when we stumble.

PRAY OVER IT

Dear God, Thank you that You are quick to forgive my sins. I praise You for being a Mighty Redeemer. But I confess that, sometimes, I don't take my sin as seriously as I should. I want to avoid sin like I would avoid any other danger, and I want to be quick to come back into fellowship with You. When I fall, help me to know how to quickly recover and restore the joy of fellowship. In Jesus' Name, Amen.

DAY 1

THE PROBLEM OF SIN

PONDER IT

If you call your sins mistakes, then you will never deal with them as sins. In order to understand how to restore our fellowship with God after we sin, we have to understand sin. We need to call sin what it is.

Sin is an affront to a holy God, and if you call sin by some other name—a misjudgment, a malfunction, a mistake, or a sickness—you cannot have fellowship with God.

The world tries to explain our sin as a lack of knowledge or enlightenment, defective genes, or environmental flaws. All of these terms remove the personal responsibility of wrongdoing. In fact, many of us don't see ourselves as sinners needing to be forgiven, but as people who make mistakes and need to be fixed. Therefore, we try to fix ourselves through religion and psychology and self-actualization.

However, the problem is sin, and it can only be forgiven, not fixed. God made a way through His Son Jesus for our sins to be forgiven, and unless we can acknowledge our misjudgments and mistakes as sin, we cannot be forgiven. God judges or forgives our sin when we agree with Him that it is indeed sin.

The world might do its best to remove the feeling of guilt, but no doctor, psychologist, friend, or self-help book can actually remove guilt— only Jesus can. Through Jesus, God forgives, cleanses, and forgets our sin.

> "For I will be merciful to their unrighteousness, and their sins and their lawless deeds I will remember no more" (Hebrews 8:12).

> "I, even I, am He who blots out your transgressions for My own sake; and I will not remember your sins" (Isaiah 43:25).

God doesn't forget our sin intellectually because He can never truly learn or forget anything as an omniscient being. But He doesn't hold our sins against us anymore; He remembers them as forgiven sins. They are buried in the grave of God's forgetfulness. When you are saved, all your sins are forgiven and gone (see Isaiah 1:18).

Your past, present, and future sins will never be brought up against you anymore. Your past is forgiven, but your future is also secure. Though our sin is forgiven and forgotten when we are saved, we can distort the fellowship we have with God by failing to repent of our sin.

> **If we say that we have fellowship with Him, and walk in darkness, we lie and do not practice the truth. But if we walk in the light as He is in the light, we have fellowship with one another, and the blood of Jesus Christ His Son cleanses us from all sin (1 John 1:6-7).**

A son cannot lose his sonship by disobeying his parents, but he can change the fellowship he has with his mother and father. A daughter can displease her parents without being disowned. Sonship is once for all, but fellowship changes. Sonship is fixed by birth, but fellowship is determined when we choose to obey or disobey our Father's instructions. In the same way, our sin breaks our fellowship with God.

PUT IT IN WRITING

- What cultural lies about sin do you hear in society today? What other names does the world call "sin"?
- Why do we need to keep repenting of our sin, even though it was already forgiven when we were saved?

> If you say that man is ill, but not evil,
> weak, but not wicked, and sick,
> but not sinful, then you will never
> deal with your sin as you should.
>
> ADRIAN ROGERS

DAY 2

EXPOSE YOUR SIN

PONDER IT

If you are saved, your sin will never be brought up against you in order to condemn you and cast you into Hell. But your sin can interrupt fellowship with the Father. We need a formula for fellowship. We need to know that we are right before God, and if we are not, we need to know how to get back into fellowship.

Your sin must be exposed to the light. Notice that John repeats the phrase "if we say" several times in 1 John 1.

> **If we say that we have fellowship with Him, and walk in darkness, we lie and do not practice the truth (v. 6).**
>
> **If we say that we have no sin, we deceive ourselves, and the truth is not in us (v. 8).**
>
> **If we say that we have not sinned, we make Him a liar, and His word is not in us (v. 10).**

John was addressing people who denied their sin. When a child of God harbors sin in his heart, he may begin to lie to other people. The sin of a person who is saved is forgiven and forgotten. But if sin creeps into the believer's life, it is tempting to pretend that nothing is wrong, especially around Christians who might call him out. He will lie to cover up the truth of his sin.

We also deceive ourselves when we deny our sin. If you tell a lie long enough, eventually you believe it's true. You will become a spiritual hypocrite, and this false life can lead to depression and mental breakdown. We break our fellowship with God when we lie to Him and refuse to admit our sin. If the Holy Spirit convicts us that something is a sin, we make God a liar when we do it anyway. Concealing our sin is the most dangerous thing we can do.

You can avoid this spiral of lies by exposing your sin to the light. We do not confess our sin to be condemned or to wallow in self-pity, but to be cleansed and restore the joy of fellowship with God. Light reveals what is wrong; it highlights imperfections. We do this by asking the Holy Spirit to search our hearts and make us aware of any wicked ways. We ask Him to convict us of our sin, to open our hearts in humility, and to help us repent. When we do this, we walk in the light of fellowship with God and with one another.

PUT IT IN WRITING

- What are the consequences of hiding our sin? What are the effects on ourselves, on others in our lives, and on our relationship with God?
- What sin in your life needs to be brought into the light? What do you hide from others? Write down a prayer, asking the Holy Spirit to convict you, humble you, and lead you back into fellowship with God.

> An excuse is just the skin of a reason stuffed with a lie.
>
> ADRIAN ROGERS

DAY 3

ASK THE HOLY SPIRIT TO CONVICT YOU OF SIN

▪ PONDER IT

As you seek to expose your sin to the light, you must ask the Holy Spirit to convict you of sin. But there is a difference between the Holy Spirit's conviction and Satan's accusation. The Holy Spirit of God *convicts* you of sin, but the devil *accuses* you of sin. Both bring awareness to the existence of your sin, but there is a distinct difference in how they want you to respond to it. Here are some ways to know the difference between the two:

- **The Holy Spirit convicts us of legitimate sin.** He brings information to our minds about sin that must be exposed. When the devil whispers accusations, he makes illegitimate claims about sin that is already gone and forgiven. Satan brings condemnation and shame; the Holy Spirit brings legitimate guilt and reminds us that forgiveness is available (see 1 John 1:9).
- **The Holy Spirit convicts you specifically.** If Satan cannot accuse you of a specific sin that is already forgiven, he will make you feel a general sense of guilt. He'll convince you that you are vile, unworthy, unlovable and up to no good. He loves to give people a negative self-view. But the Holy Spirit doesn't convict us generally; He convicts us specifically. Satan will tell you lies that make you feel bad all over. But the Holy Spirit is like a skilled surgeon who puts a finger on the sore spot, making you aware of exactly what is wrong. He calls our sin by name.

  Do not confess your sin in generalities; confess the specifics and name your sin. True confession is not "Lord, I sinned. Forgive me." If you've watched something you shouldn't have, taken something that wasn't yours, lied to someone, or spoken cruelly, call it what it is. When we do this, God's cleansing floods in, changing us and sanctifying us. This is the only way we can change and sin less.

- **The Holy Spirit of God will convict you redemptively.** He convicts with a purpose to restore fellowship with God. When God deals with you as a son or daughter, He's not trying to get even with you; He is trying to restore you to fellowship. He hates it when the fellowship is broken, so He names the sin that caused a wedge between you so that He can forgive and cleanse you. The devil accuses you destructively, to drive you to despair and away from God. But the conviction of the Holy Spirit draws you to confession and forgiveness and fellowship.

Open up your heart to the Holy Spirit of God, and ask Him to expose it to the light. Ask the Lord to show you if there is any unconfessed, unforsaken, unforgiven sin in your life. The Holy Spirit will legitimately, specifically, and redemptively tell you where the problem is.

PUT IT IN WRITING

- When have you experienced the Holy Spirit's conviction and Satan's accusations? How could you tell the difference between the two?
- Is there any legitimate, specific sin that the Holy Spirit has brought to mind today? What is your next step of faith?

> Better to die with conviction
> than to live with compromise.
>
> ADRIAN ROGERS

DAY 4

CONFESS YOUR SIN

■ PONDER IT

After the Holy Spirit convicts us of our sin and brings it to the light, we need to take the next step in the formula for fellowship: we must express it to the Lord.

> **If we confess our sins, He is faithful and just to forgive us our sins and to cleanse us from all unrighteousness (1 John 1:9).**

A confession of sin is not just an admission of sin; it is an agreement with God about that sin. To confess your sin means to name it and nail it to the cross. You agree with the Holy Spirit that you have sinned and something needs to change.

Here are some specific ways to confess sin to the Lord:

- **Do it immediately.** The word "confess" is in the present tense. Don't save up your sins for the end of the week or even for the end of the day. As soon as the Holy Spirit brings awareness to an area of sin in your life, confess it.
- **Take immediate action to remove it.** When you have a speck of dust in your eye, you don't wait to remove it. You take it out as quickly as possible. This is how you should respond to sin in your life. Deal with it immediately.
- **Confess with the confidence that you are already forgiven.** We can be certain that God is faithful and just to forgive us our sins (see 1 John 1:9). Jesus died for all our sins; we have the ability to be completely cleansed.

When we are cleansed, we restore fellowship with God and fellowship with one another.

PUT IT IN WRITING

- Which part of confession is the most difficult for you?
- Are you quick to bring your sins to God? Why or why not?

> You cannot confess to God what
> you will not admit to yourself.
>
> ADRIAN ROGERS

DAY 5

A SPIRIT-FILLED LIFE

PONDER IT

We have learned that as we expose our sin to the light, the Holy Spirit convicts us legitimately and specifically. He brings up new sin that is festering in our hearts, and He names it. He tells us exactly what needs to change. Then we have an opportunity to confess our sin to the Lord. Through this process of acknowledging and repenting of sin, the Holy Spirit transforms our hearts and our lives.

The Spirit-filled life is not a life in which you can never sin. John wrote these words to people who were already believers.

> **If we say that we have no sin, we deceive ourselves, and the truth is not in us (1 John 1:8).**

As Christians, we become aware of our sin, quickly confess it, and get right back up. We serve a God who picks us up when we are down. When we are saved, He doesn't condemn us when we fail, but graciously brings awareness to our sin and calls us back into fellowship with Himself. He loves us too much to leave us in our messes. He wants us to experience the fullness of joy through a life lived in holiness and fellowship with Him.

If the Holy Spirit has brought awareness to an area of sin in your life this week, thank Him for His graciousness in exposing your sin to the light. Next, bring that sin in confession before the Lord. Experience the cleansing of the Gospel of Jesus Christ, and enjoy the restoration of fellowship with God and others.

- **PUT IT IN WRITING**
  - What has the Holy Spirit shown you about your sin this week? What is your next step of faith?

> You know how your mouth feels when you brush your teeth in the morning? You feel that way all over when you are cleansed by the power of Jesus.
>
> ADRIAN ROGERS

DAY 6

A FORMULA FOR FELLOWSHIP

PRACTICE IT

Confess sin immediately, specifically, and confidently. That is the formula for fellowship.

You might not yet have a relationship with Jesus. You might not have the assurance that all of your sin is forgiven once and for all. If you would like to, you can be saved and receive the forgiveness and cleansing that comes with being a son or daughter of God. All you need to do is believe in the life, death, and resurrection of Jesus Christ. Agree with God that you are a sinner. Turn from your sin and confess Jesus as Lord. He will change you from the inside out. He will break the grip of sin on your life and bring you into the joy of fellowship with Himself.

If you would like to accept Jesus as your Lord and Savior, pray and receive His salvation through faith. Then thank Him for doing it, and rejoice that you are living as a new creation in Christ!

PROCLAIM IT

Share your next step of faith with a trusted friend or mentor. Ask that person to join you in praying what God is asking you to do.

If you prayed to receive Christ, please share your decision with another Christian you know or with your pastor. We would also like to hear about it, so that we can provide you with free resources to help you grow in your new faith. Please let us know by going to **lwf.org/discover-jesus**, scrolling down the page and clicking on *I Believe*.

Life is short; death is sure.
Sin is the curse; Christ is the cure.

ADRIAN ROGERS

When we were born again, we were born to win.

ADRIAN ROGERS

WEEK 9

HOW DO I KNOW GOD IS WORKING IN MY LIFE?

■ INTRODUCTION

One ingredient in nearly every food we consume is a deadly poison. We put it in our oatmeal, on our pasta, in soups, and on nearly everything that can be cooked. It is chlorine, which is half of the chemical makeup of table salt.

Thankfully, chlorine is not dangerous to us when combined with sodium, which makes the delicious flavor enhancer that sits on our dining room tables. The Gospel of Christ functions in the same way. It is life and hope to some, while to others, who choose not to believe in Jesus, it means judgment and death.

Just as pharmacists compound together various powders, chemicals, and minerals to create the medicines that bring healing to our bodies, the saving chemistry of the cross is also made up of many parts. This week, we will study Romans 8:28 and take a closer look at how the Gospel of Jesus Christ seasons everything in our lives—the good and the bad.

> **And we know that all things work together for good to those who love God, to those who are the called according to His purpose (Romans 8:28).**

■ PRAY OVER IT

Dear God, I want to believe that all things are working together for good, but sometimes the circumstances of my life don't seem good. Help me to understand the beautiful chemistry of the cross. Give me eyes to see Your hand at work in my life, and faith to believe that You are over all things. In Jesus' Name, Amen.

DAY 1

THE WORK OF THE CROSS IS CERTAIN AND COMPLETE

PONDER IT

The Gospel's work is certain. Paul's meaning in this verse is clear and he says that we can know this is true.

> And we know that all things work together for good (Romans 8:28a).

No matter how bad life might seem or what circumstances may arise, God promised that through the cross, He would work all things together for His glory and for the good of those who love Him. One thing God cannot do is lie. God's promises are certain.

The Gospel is a complete work. Paul said that not *some* things or *most* things, but *all* things work together for good.

It's obvious that the positive things in our lives work together for good. When we experience good things, it glorifies God and edifies our spirits. Contrary to what we may think or feel, even the sorrowful things work together for our good.

Consider how God dealt with the people of Judah in 2 Kings 25. He allowed them to be exiled to Babylon, a brutal, foreign land. Still, God used these difficult circumstances for their benefit.

> "I acknowledge those who are carried away captive from Judah, whom I have sent out of this place for their own good..." (Jeremiah 24:5b).

David, who was even called a man after God's own heart, had a tendency to stray from the Lord. In a time when God made David sick, he wrote these words:

> It is good for me that I have been afflicted, that I may learn Your statutes (Psalm 119:71).

Sometimes a sick bed can teach us more than a sermon because hardship gets our attention away from ourselves and onto God.

Joseph, a beloved son and faithful man, was put in a pit by his brothers, sold as a slave, and put in prison as an innocent man. But God used this adversity to make him prime minister of Egypt. Ultimately, Joseph helped save the Jews during a time of famine. He said this to his brothers:

> **But as for you, you meant evil against me; but God meant it for good, in order to bring it about as it is this day, to save many people alive (Genesis 50:20).**

A king named Manasseh had difficulty serving God, so God allowed him to fall into the ruthless captivity of the Assyrians.

> **Now when he was in affliction, he implored the Lord his God, and humbled himself greatly before the God of his fathers, and prayed to Him; and He received his entreaty, heard his supplication, and brought him back to Jerusalem into his kingdom. Then Manasseh knew that the Lord was God (2 Chronicles 33:12-13).**

Manasseh's iron chains were a greater blessing to him than his golden crown. He cried out in the midst of his anguish, and God responded.

You might have been hurt by someone. You might be sick, grieving a loss, or navigating a bad relationship. But you can know that God uses everything meant for evil for our good. He is a mighty Redeemer.

PUT IT IN WRITING

- When you look back on a sorrowful experience from your past, can you see how God used it for something good? Explain.
- What does Romans 8:28 imply about God's character? What do the stories of people in the Bible tell us about the way God works?

DAY 2

GOD IS SOVEREIGN

▪ PONDER IT

A poor, old woman lived alone in a little apartment. She loved God, but her landlord was not saved and often ridiculed her for her faith. One day, the landlord overheard her praying for food because she didn't have enough money for groceries. Thinking he could cure her from her religious superstitions, he went out, bought a basket of groceries, and left them at her door. When she found the groceries, she praised the Lord for His faithfulness!

A little while later, her landlord knocked at the door. She answered, saying, "You say there's no God, but look! I prayed for groceries, and God graciously provided them for me when I had nothing."

His lips twisted in a cynical smile, and he said, "You poor, foolish woman. I heard you pray for those groceries, and I bought them for you. God didn't give you anything!"

She replied, "You are the fool. I asked God for groceries, and I got groceries, even if God sent them through the devil."

You know that positive things work together for good, and that even our difficulties can bring good things. But have you considered that even satanic things work together for good?

Paul had an affliction he couldn't remove, which he called a "messenger of Satan" (see 2 Corinthians 12:7). God allowed this to happen, and even Satan unwittingly became the servant of God.

This doesn't mean that we should willingly sin. If you're bound to sin, you're bound to suffer. But even that suffering will work together for your good. The Bible says that even the wrath of man will praise God (see Psalm 76:10), and that where sin abounds, grace abounds even more (see Romans 5:20).

Before the crucifixion of Jesus, Simon Peter boasted that he would go with Christ both to prison and to death. But then Jesus prophesied that Peter would deny Him three times that night. Even though Jesus knew Peter would betray Him, He also knew redemption was coming.

And the Lord said, "Simon, Simon! Indeed, Satan has asked for you, that he may sift you as wheat. But I have prayed for you, that your faith should not fail; and when you have returned to Me, strengthen your brethren" (Luke 22:31-32).

After Peter's denial, Jesus forgave and restored him. Even through Peter's disobedience, God took his sin and used it for His glory.

Now no chastening seems to be joyful for the present, but painful; nevertheless, afterward it yields the peaceable fruit of righteousness to those who have been trained by it (Hebrews 12:11).

Our blessings, friendships, victories, losses, sorrows, and sins all work together for our good when we are in Christ. God is sovereign, and His redemptive work on the cross is certain and complete.

PUT IT IN WRITING

- How does Simon Peter's messy story encourage your faith?
- What does it tell you about God that He uses everything, including the work of the devil, for good? How does this affect how you view the difficult things you are currently facing?

> God is sovereign, so live confidently.
> God is holy, so live reverently.
>
> ADRIAN ROGERS

DAY 3

THE CAUSE

■ PONDER IT

God is the cause for the work in our lives. The New International Version translates Romans 8:28 this way:

> **And we know that in all things *God works* for the good of those who love him (Romans 8:28a, emphasis added).**

In Him also we have obtained an inheritance, being predestined according to the purpose of Him who works all things according to the counsel of His will (Ephesians 1:11).

Martin Luther, the leader of the Protestant Reformation, struggled with depression and sadness. Though he loved God, sometimes he focused on outward circumstances. He sat in his room sulking. His wife Katharina would try to get him to come out to no avail.

One day, Katharina walked into his room dressed in all black as if she were going to a funeral.

Martin Luther asked, "Katharina, who died?"

She replied, "Haven't you heard? God is dead!"

He said, "God is not dead; that's blasphemy!"

"And it's blasphemy for you to be living like He is dead," Katharina said.

Martin Luther got the message and repented. Afterwards, he wrote the famous hymn "A Mighty Fortress is our God," which states, "A mighty fortress is our God, a bulwark never failing; our helper he, amid the flood of mortal ills prevailing."

Martin Luther recognized God's sovereignty, or full control, over our lives. God causes His will to happen. His will is to work all things for our good.

PUT IT IN WRITING

- What did you learn about God's character today? How do Romans 8:28 and Ephesians 1:11 change your perspective?
- In what ways do you, like Martin Luther, live like God is dead? What would you do differently if you truly believed that God causes all things to work together for good?

> If the outlook seems glum, I want to tell you the uplook is very bright!
>
> ADRIAN ROGERS

DAY 4

THE CONDITIONS

■ **PONDER IT**

The promise that all things work together for good is conditional. Romans 8:28 is not a promise for everyone.

> **And we know that all things work together for good to those who love God, *to those who are the called according to His purpose* (Romans 8:28, emphasis added).**

God only works all things for good for those who love Him. The reverse of Romans 8:28 is also true: all things work together for bad for those who do not love God. Unsaved people might experience the best of life's luxuries, but if Jesus is not their Lord and Savior, their lives will ultimately end in ruin.

It is dangerous for those who reject Christ to come to church. When they hear the truth of the Gospel and dismiss it, they choose destruction.

> **For we are to God the fragrance of Christ among those who are being saved and among those who are perishing. To the one we are the aroma of death leading to death, and to the other the aroma of life leading to life (2 Corinthians 2:15-16).**

The Gospel exposes every sin.

> **For the word of God is living and powerful, and sharper than any two-edged sword, piercing even to the division of soul and spirit, and of joints and marrow, and is a discerner of the thoughts and intents of the heart (Hebrews 4:12).**

The more truth non-Christians reject, the greater judgment they will receive.

> "And whoever will not receive you nor hear your words, when you depart from that house or city, shake off the dust from your feet. Assuredly, I say to you, it will be more tolerable for the land of Sodom and Gomorrah in the day of judgment than for that city" (Matthew 10:14-15)!

Jesus compared Himself to a door (see John 10:7-10). Doors keep people in, but they also keep people out. Those who love Him are let in, but because of His righteousness and holiness, He will keep out those who refuse Him.

The resurrection of Christ is assurance that judgment is coming, and it requires people to choose sides. Paul spoke about this when he preached to unbelievers in Athens.

> Truly, these times of ignorance God overlooked, but now commands all men everywhere to repent, because He has appointed a day on which He will judge the world in righteousness by the Man whom He has ordained. He has given assurance of this to all by raising Him from the dead (Acts 17:30-31).

The assurance of judgment is the resurrection of Jesus. The same God that raised up Jesus Christ is the God that will raise you up and bring you to judgment. The resurrection either redeems your soul or seals your doom.

All things work together for good to those who love God, and all things work together for bad to those who are not called according to His purposes.

PUT IT IN WRITING

- The strange thing about the Gospel is that it is offered to everyone, but not everyone will receive it. What does it tell you about God that the promise of Romans 8:28 is only available to those who believe and receive the Gospel?
- The condition of Romans 8:28 should motivate us to share the Gospel with those who are not saved. Who in your sphere of influence can you share Jesus with this week?

DAY 5

THE CONSEQUENCES

▧ PONDER IT

Jesus' work on the cross has consequences for those who believe. We often trivialize what Romans 8:28 really means, thinking it means that we will reap earthly pleasures. We hear "our good" and think of restful vacations, promotions at work, material comforts, and things that feel good on this side of Heaven. This is not what Paul meant.

> **For whom He foreknew, He also predestined *to be conformed to the image of His Son*, that He might be the firstborn among many brethren (Romans 8:29, emphasis added).**

Our good is not caught up in our physical health, wealth, or happiness. Our good is to become more like Jesus. The best possible thing that could happen to us is that we would conform to the image of God's Son. The more we recognize this and spend time in fellowship with God, the more we begin to find pleasure in being like Him.

People can be unsaved, and everything might still go their way. They might think that they don't need God because they have everything they want. They have esteemed jobs, flashy homes and cars, and attractive spouses; they boast on social media about how exciting their lives are. But even if bad things don't catch up to them during their lifetimes, they will perish and spend eternity apart from God in Hell. They can have all the fun they want on Earth, but all things will ultimately work together for their bad.

The devil always gives the best first, but Jesus always saves the best for last. When Jesus turned water into wine, the master of the feast said:

> **"Every man at the beginning sets out the good wine, and when the guests have well drunk, then the inferior. You have kept the good wine until now" (John 2:10).**

We must be patient. The positive consequence of loving God is that we grow more and more into His likeness, and one day, we will be glorified with Jesus Christ in Heaven. This is the good work that God does in the life of the believer—the chemistry of the work of the cross.

> As was the man of dust, so also are those who are of the dust, and as is the heavenly Man, so also are those who are heavenly. And as we have borne the image of the man of dust, we shall also bear the image of the heavenly man (1 Corinthians 15:48-49).

> But we all, with unveiled face, beholding as in a mirror the glory of the Lord, are being transformed into the same image from glory to glory, just as by the Spirit of the Lord (2 Corinthians 3:18).

▪ PUT IT IN WRITING

- How has your perspective of Romans 8:28 changed this week? Have you learned anything about the meaning of "our good"?
- How does it encourage your faith to know that God saves the best for last?

> The devil always gives the best first, but Jesus always saves the best for last.
>
> ADRIAN ROGERS

DAY 6

THE CHEMISTRY OF THE CROSS

PRACTICE IT

The redemptive work of the cross is life to those who love Jesus. By His grace, His death and resurrection made a way for us to not only spend eternity with Him in Heaven but also to grow into His likeness here on Earth.

Romans 8:28 shows us that the Gospel means that all things work together for good to all Christians. The Gospel's work is complete and certain. God is the One who causes all things to work together for good, but this promise is conditional. It is for those who love God and receive His Son as Lord and Savior. There are consequences for believing in the Gospel. They may not all be pleasant, but they are all for our ultimate good.

If you would like to be included in the promise God made in Romans 8:28, surrendering your life to Jesus Christ, you can right now. God desires that none should perish (see 2 Peter 3:9), and He wants to work all things together for your good. Pray, repenting of your sin, and believing in the sinless life, sacrificial death, and victorious resurrection of Jesus Christ. Come under His Lordship. Then thank Him for the free gift of salvation that you have received.

◾ PROCLAIM IT

If you love God, thank Him for working all things together for your good. Tell someone in your life who has not been saved about the chemistry of the cross and invite that person to receive the promise of God.

If you prayed to receive Christ, please share your decision with another Christian you know or with your pastor. We would also like to hear about it, so that we can provide you with free resources to help you grow in your new faith. Please let us know by going to **lwf.org/discover-jesus**, scrolling down the page and clicking on *I Believe*.

> Jesus didn't come to make you a nicer person. He came to radically, dramatically, and eternally transform you.
>
> ADRIAN ROGERS

LISTEN NOW

Use the QR code below to listen to the original messages from Pastor Adrian Rogers' series, *Back to the Basics, Volume 1*. Each message in the list corresponds to a chapter in this Bible Study.

lwf.org/audio-cda137

How Can You Be Certain the Bible Is the Word of God

How to Be Saved and Know It

How You Can Be Sure You Are Eternally Secure

Eternal Security: A Scriptural Defense

How to Have a Spirit-Filled Life

How to Turn Temptations Into Triumphs

How to Come Back When You're Down

A Formula for Fellowship

The Chemistry of the Cross

DISCUSSION GUIDE

GROUNDED IN TRUTH

VOLUME 1

This study is based on a message series Pastor Rogers preached on the basic beliefs of the Christian faith. Whether you have a group of people exploring the Christian faith, young believers, or mature believers, this study goes back to the basics to give everyone a firm foundation for their faith so they can live grounded in truth.

KEY QUESTIONS ADDRESSED IN THIS STUDY

- How can I be saved?
- Is the Bible true?
- How can I know I'm going to Heaven?
- How do I deal with temptations and sin as a believer?
- How should I live as a Christian?

KEY CONCEPTS

- Anyone can be saved and know they are going to Heaven.
- We can trust that God's Word is inspired and true.
- Believers can still be tempted and sin, but they also can ask for forgiveness to restore their fellowship with God.

PREPARING TO LEAD/FACILITATE EACH SESSION

Read through the weekly lesson in the Bible study and spend time writing your answers to the questions. Encourage the group participants to do the same. Before the session, review the **Discussion Questions** and the **Prayer & Action Point**. The questions are meant to build and increase in depth. If you have time, listen to Pastor Rogers' sermon for each week. He includes additional information and interesting stories that may not be included in the text of the Bible study. When appropriate, you may want to invite your group to listen to specific sections of Pastor Rogers' sermons.

CONDUCTING EACH SESSION

At the beginning of each session, read the **Introduction** from the Bible Study book to your group, then open discussion by asking participants to share their biggest questions or takeaways from the week. Please keep in mind that you do not have to have the answers to the questions people ask. Sometimes the act of asking the question is helpful, and having a safe place to be curious about our faith is important. Allow the group to answer the question or commit to finding the answers together before the next session. If specific questions are too far off the topic of the study, you may want to meet with the person asking those questions outside the session or get the support of a pastor or church leader.

Next, pray and ask God to guide your conversation and then lead your group through the **Discussion Questions**. Your role is to facilitate the lessons and the conversation. Make sure everyone has an opportunity to share. Avoid the temptation to fill silence with talking or lecturing. The silence can allow time for everyone to process, think, and listen to the Holy Spirit. You can also invite participants to go deeper by asking questions like "Why? Why not?" or saying "Tell me more." You can ask someone to clarify an answer by saying "Can you help me understand…?"

The questions are intentionally ordered so that the first two questions are typically questions that everyone can answer. They are meant to get people talking. If you want to keep them talking, avoid fixing and judging. Do not try to fix their problems or tell them what they are doing wrong. If others in the group try to do this, find a polite way to bring the focus back to sharing personal experiences.

The questions will increase in depth. You can jump around based on which questions feel the most applicable to your group. Be listening to the Holy Spirit as well to see if other questions come to mind. As the facilitator, you are listening to the group and the Holy Spirit at the same time. Your situation each week can change based on participant feedback and questions. You are leading your group as God is leading you. Stay focused on the content and the context of the study, but also be attentive to where the Spirit is moving.

The last question asks group members to apply what they have learned to their lives. You may invite participants to silently reflect or write down their answers until they are more comfortable in the group. If people share their answers out loud, avoid judgment statements that are positive or negative. This will help people avoid comparison and people pleasing. Simply say, "Thank you for sharing" or "We will be praying for that with you."

Encourage participants to find one or two other people with whom to discuss the **Prayer & Action Point**. It is meant to challenge them to apply the main teaching in the lesson in a practical way and open the door for accountability. Participants can share their answers to the question and then pray for each other. Remember to affirm the importance of confidentiality within the group as participants share.

WEEK 1

HOW CAN I BE CERTAIN ABOUT THE WORD OF GOD?

LISTEN TO THE MESSAGE
lwf.org/audio-1725

DISCUSSION QUESTIONS

1. What was your biggest takeaway from this week's study? What questions do you have after going through the study?
2. When you were younger, what were you taught about the Bible and where it came from? What do you know or believe about the Bible today?
3. How are the Bible and science related? Do you have to let go of science in order to be a Christian?
4. What have you heard people use to challenge the historical accuracy of the Bible? What has your research revealed?
5. What is the benefit of using multiple authors in different time periods and locations to write the Scripture?
6. What are the biblical themes you consistently see throughout Scripture? Do the inaccuracies people often claim exist change any of those major themes?
7. From Day 5, which role of Scripture applies to you most this week: saving for the sinner, sanctifying for the saint, sufficient for the sufferer, and satisfying for the scholar? Why?

PRAYER & ACTION POINT

As a group, thank God for the gift of His Word and ask Him to use it to teach you as you go through this study. The Word of God is alive, and different people walk away with different applications for their lives. Allow space for this diversity within your group and trust the Holy Spirit to reveal God's truth. If you continue to have questions about God's Word, seek the guidance of your small group leader or pastor.

WEEK 2

HOW CAN I BE SAVED?

◾ LISTEN TO THE MESSAGE
lwf.org/audio-1726

◾ DISCUSSION QUESTIONS
1. What was your biggest takeaway from this week's study? What questions do you have after going through the study?
2. Almost every religion gives a path to a good afterlife. What are some of the ways other religions say you can have a good afterlife?
3. Is having doubts about your faith a bad thing? What is the purpose of doubt (see Day 1 of the study)?
4. What is the difference between knowing something is true and believing it is true?
5. One of the key tenets of the Christian faith that is not shared by any other faith is the belief that you don't need to earn your salvation; it is a free gift from God. Why do some people, even those who are Christians, want to believe that we have to earn our salvation through good works?
6. What is the benefit of being saved by faith and not by works? How does this impact the way Christians live their lives?
7. What part of your life are you holding onto because you are afraid of giving it to Jesus Christ or letting Him into that part? What would it look like to make Him the Lord of your life?

◾ PRAYER & ACTION POINT
With a partner, confess the ways you have been trying to earn your salvation or the areas of your life you have not given to Jesus Christ. Remind each other of God's grace and pray for one another.

WEEK 3

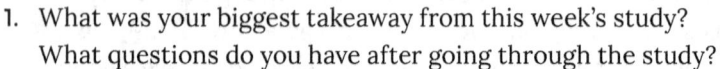

HOW CAN I BE SURE I AM SAVED?

LISTEN TO THE MESSAGE

lwf.org/audio-1728

DISCUSSION QUESTIONS

1. What was your biggest takeaway from this week's study? What questions do you have after going through the study?
2. What were some of the fears that are keeping you or have kept you from making a decision for Christ? What were you afraid you would have to start doing or stop doing if you were a Christian?
3. What are some of the things that make you wonder if you are really going to Heaven?
4. Which of the points (see the words that start with "p" on Days 3-5) were the most meaningful to you? How do they address your doubts about your salvation?
5. How does what you believe about your relationship with God reflect what you ultimately believe about God? What aspect of God's character do you need to remember?
6. How does knowing you are eternally secure impact your daily life? Does this mean that you can sin more?
7. Where do you see the Holy Spirit working in your life? What is the "good work" He is doing in you and through you?

PRAYER & ACTION POINT

With a partner, identify one of the verses from this week's study to memorize. Share with your partner why you chose that verse and pray for one another.

WEEK 4

HOW CAN I KNOW I AM GOING TO HEAVEN?

LISTEN TO THE MESSAGE
lwf.org/audio-1729

DISCUSSION QUESTIONS

1. What was your biggest takeaway from this week's study? What questions do you have after going through the study?
2. Do you know people who used to consider themselves Christians but no longer claim Christ? What are some of the reasons they have given for walking away from Christianity?
3. According to Day 1, what was the difference between Judas and the prodigal son? How do their external actions reflect their internal or spiritual state?
4. According to Day 4, how is the person who "samples" the Gospel and doesn't believe different from the person who never heard the Gospel?
5. Have you ever felt like God doesn't love you or has rejected you? Have you ever denied knowing Jesus like Peter did? Have you ever had a time when you felt God was holding onto you even if you weren't holding on to Him?
6. Before you were saved, what held you back from believing? What has your faith cost you?
7. What is the fruit of your life? How do you stay connected to Jesus, the true vine?

PRAYER & ACTION POINT

With a partner, share about your spiritual journey. Share the pieces of your story that God used to help you understand the Gospel. Share any doubts you have about your salvation and pray for one another.

WEEK 5

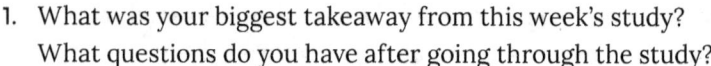

HOW CAN I LIVE A SPIRIT-FILLED LIFE?

LISTEN TO THE MESSAGE
lwf.org/audio-1733

DISCUSSION QUESTIONS

1. What was your biggest takeaway from this week's study? What questions do you have after going through the study?
2. What was your favorite car you have owned or what is your dream car? What do you know about the engine?
3. When was the last time you treated someone in such a way that you knew the Holy Spirit was working? When have you treated someone differently than what comes naturally?
4. How would other people describe your work ethic? Do you treat your work like Jesus is your boss?
5. How is your worship and your witness? What are the spiritual battles you or those close to you are facing?
6. On Day 4, which aspect do you feel you embrace and which one is challenging for you—completely committed, continual control, or claiming the fullness?
7. What is the evidence in your life of adoration, appreciation, or accommodation?

PRAYER & ACTION POINT

As a group, spend time in prayer practicing adoration, telling God why you love Him, and appreciation, thanking God for what He has done. Spend time praying for one another as you seek to follow the Holy Spirit more closely.

WEEK 6

HOW CAN I TURN TEMPTATIONS INTO TRIUMPHS?

LISTEN TO THE MESSAGE

lwf.org/audio-1732

DISCUSSION QUESTIONS

1. What was your biggest takeaway from this week's study? What questions do you have after going through the study?
2. What role does marketing, social media, or entertainment play in temptation in our society? Do these temptations come from the world, the flesh, or the devil?
3. In the past, how have you dealt with temptation: by giving into it, by fighting it in your own strength, or by overcoming it through the power of Christ?
4. Why does God allow us to be tempted? If you could never choose to sin, could you really choose to follow Christ?
5. When you think about what is tempting you, which category does it fall under: the lust of the eyes, the lust of the flesh, or the pride of life?
6. Why is it impossible to fight temptation apart from Jesus Christ?
7. How has God helped you overcome temptation in the past? What did it look like for you to flee, have faith, and fight?

PRAYER & ACTION POINT

With a partner, share a temptation you are facing or confess a sin you have given into. Sin grows in the darkness of secrets, silence, and shame. Sharing with just one other person can bring the sin into the light to allow forgiveness and healing. Remind each other of the forgiveness Jesus offers and pray for one another.

WEEK 7

HOW DO I DEAL WITH SIN IN MY LIFE?

LISTEN TO THE MESSAGE
lwf.org/audio-1730

DISCUSSION QUESTIONS

1. What was your biggest takeaway from this week's study? What questions do you have after going through the study?
2. What was something you tried to get away with as a child or a teenager? Were you successful or did you get caught?
3. If all of our sins are already forgiven, why should believers try to avoid sin?
4. Which of the effects of sin stood out to you the most this week? Were any of them new ideas for you?
5. Are you confident God still loves you even though you are not perfect?
6. Why is confession an important part of the process? What is God's posture toward us when we confess our sin?
7. Have you received cleansing for your sin or are you still feeling guilty for something God has forgotten? What needs to happen for you to let go of your past sin?

PRAYER & ACTION POINT

On your own, spend time confessing your sin to God and receiving His forgiveness. You may want to make a list and then destroy it as a physical reminder that the sin has been paid for.

WEEK 8

HOW DO I RESTORE FELLOWSHIP WITH GOD?

LISTEN TO THE MESSAGE
lwf.org/audio-1731

DISCUSSION QUESTIONS

1. What was your biggest takeaway from this week's study? What questions do you have after going through the study?
2. What are the things in life you are afraid of?
3. What are some ways our society encourages us to minimize or normalize sin?
4. Why is bringing sin into the light terrifying for most people? Why are the benefits of bringing sin into the light?
5. How do you know the difference between the Holy Spirit's conviction and Satan's accusations? When the Holy Spirit has convicted you of sin, how does it feel or what does it sound like in your mind?
6. What are the benefits of confessing sin immediately, taking action to remove it, and confessing with confidence? How has this process helped you grow spiritually or change bad habits?
7. What has the Holy Spirit shown you about your sin this week? What is your next step of faith?

PRAYER & ACTION POINT

With a partner, spend a few minutes confessing your sin to one another. This will feel awkward at first, and you don't have to start with your deepest and darkest sins. Start with the sins you have committed this week that you feel comfortable sharing with someone and bringing into the light. Remind one another that all your sins are forgiven, even the ones you haven't shared. Thank God for His forgiveness, mercy, and grace, and ask Him to help you have the courage to keep bringing your sin into the light.

WEEK 9

HOW DO I KNOW GOD IS WORKING IN MY LIFE?

LISTEN TO THE MESSAGE
lwf.org/audio-1734

DISCUSSION QUESTIONS

1. What was your biggest takeaway from this week's study? What questions do you have after going through the study?
2. What is your favorite seasoning to use when cooking? Why is the same ingredient delicious to some and repulsive to others?
3. What is something unpleasant from your past that you have seen God use for good?
4. How does knowing God is sovereign provide you with perspective on the difficulties you are currently facing? What do you do to help yourself remember that He is using all things for good?
5. Do all things work together for good for everyone?
6. Read John 10:7-10. What similarities do you see between Jesus and a door? Who do you need to pray for and invite through that door?
7. How do you see yourself being transformed to be more like Jesus? How are you growing spiritually?

PRAYER & ACTION POINT

As a group, spend time thanking God for the gift of salvation and for the ways He is working in your lives. Thank Him for the good things and the hard things. Pray for one another as you face difficulties in life and pray for those who don't know Jesus.

GROUNDED IN TRUTH

Grounded in Truth, Volume 2 continues the conversation on what we believe and why we believe with chapters on:

- Why is baptism important?
- How can I have Biblical faith?
- How can I understand the Bible and apply it to my life?
- How can I identify my spiritual gifts?
- How do I know the will of God?
- How do I live a godly life?
- How can I defeat Satan's lies?
- How do I practice the presence of God?
- How do I become a mature Christian?

DISCUSSION NOTES

DISCUSSION NOTES

VISIT US ONLINE AT LWF.ORG

Love Worth Finding Ministries with Adrian Rogers is pleased to be able to bring you this Bible study. If you have found it helpful, we suggest you go to our website, **lwf.org**.

Peruse our "find answers" **Q&A** "about my life, about my world" and "about God." Sign up for an **email challenge** that brings encouragement to your inbox. Engage in a study from our **Biblical Learning Center**. Or go to the **LWF Store** for print and digital resources for yourself and those you love.

Through broadcast, print and digital media, our reach is global. Our mission is to help people find the greatest Love worth finding, Jesus Christ, and to help those who already know Jesus grow in the faith.

Put Love Worth Finding in the palm of your hand with the **MyLWF App**.

Here you'll find audio and video messages from Pastor Adrian Rogers, our daily devotional, and special programs such as our "Conversations that Matter" interview-format program on biblical topics and our "Voices" audio theater programs.

The **MyLWF App** includes programming in several languages. And you can learn how to partner in Love Worth Finding's global mission to bring people to Christ and help them grow in the faith.

Scan the QR code below or search for the heart-shaped **MyLWF App** in your favorite app store to download it today.

ADDITIONAL BIBLE STUDIES IN THIS SERIES

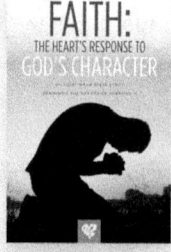

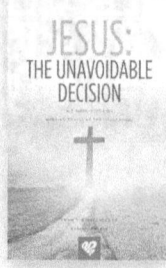

For these and other resources, visit **lwf.org**/store or call **(800) 274-5683**

www.ingramcontent.com/pod-product-compliance
Lightning Source LLC
Chambersburg PA
CBHW070528010526
44110CB00050B/2324